DORSET
Teashop Walks

DORSET
Teashop Walks

Jean Patefield

COUNTRYSIDE BOOKS
NEWBURY, BERKSHIRE

First published 1999
© Jean Patefield 1999

COUNTRYSIDE BOOKS
3 Catherine Road
Newbury, Berkshire

ISBN 1 85306 558 7

Designed by Graham Whiteman
Cover illustration by Colin Doggett
Photographs and maps by the author

Produced through MRM Associates Ltd., Reading
Typeset by Techniset Typesetters, Newton-le-Willows
Printed by J.W. Arrowsmith Ltd., Bristol

Contents

Walk

Walk

KEY TO SKETCH MAPS

Path on route	— → —	Teashop	
Path not on route	· · ·	Pub referred to in text	PH
Road	═══	Point in text	⑤
River or stream	∿∿∿	Car park	□
Sea, lake or pond		Building or feature referred to in text	▬
Summit	▲		
Church	✝	Railway	┼┼┼┼┼

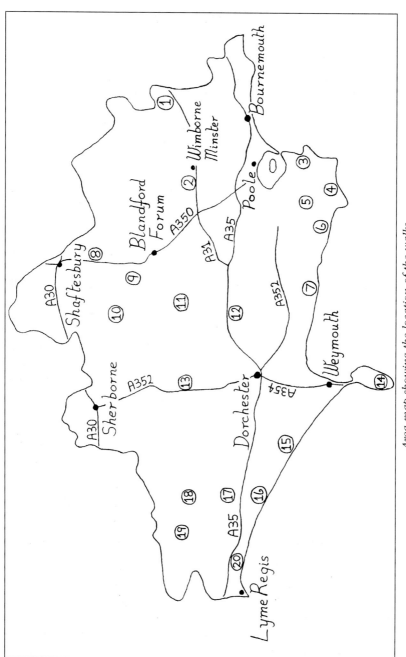

Area map showing the location of the walks

Introduction

It is literary tradition to divide places into three. Julius Caesar famously divided Gaul into three parts. Ancient Arabia was split into a desert part, a stony one and a felix or fortunate one. This portrayal has been applied to Dorset. The 'fortunate' description was given to West Dorset with its rolling hills and rich farmland. Today's visitor is just as likely to find the desert of East Dorset's heaths or the stone of Purbeck and Portland equally attractive.

The county is a delight for walkers with a diversity of scenery to be enjoyed. There is a magnificent coast which rivals anything offered by its westerly neighbours. The striking peninsula of Portland in the middle of the coastline is like nowhere else. The heart of Dorset is chalk forming rolling hills but with some steep scarp slopes. The hills are not high but have superb vantage points to be enjoyed by those who conquer them and slopes clothed in downland flowers. The more pastoral North is an enchanting patchwork of fields and hedges. Though the most important tree of hedges, the elm, has sadly succumbed to disease, there are still plenty of oaks and ancient field boundaries.

Charles II declared that he had never seen a finer county and he should have known, having seen more than most in his travels! Visitors soon surrender to the county's charms, prepared for them by numerous pictures of thatched cottages and the writings of Thomas Hardy. Above all, Dorset is a rural county with the only major conurbations being Poole, Bournemouth and Christchurch in the far east. The other towns have retained a human scale and are a pleasure to visit.

Dorset has made a major contribution to English townscapes far beyond its borders. London's noblest buildings such as St Paul's, the University tower and many others are built of Portland stone. Purbeck marble has been used in countless buildings, especially churches. The sources of these building materials are both called islands and yet neither is truly detached. The Isle of Purbeck is separated from the rest of the county by a rampart of hills. Portland is more separate but was always connected by a low strip of land covered at high tide and now more permanently attached by a causeway.

The 20 walks in this book explore the varied landscapes of Dorset. They are all between 3 and 8 miles long and should be well within the capacity of the average person, including those of mature years and families with children. They are intended to take the walker through this attractive corner of England at a gentle pace with plenty of time to stop and stare, to savour the beauty and interest all around. A dedicated yomper and stomper could

Thomas Hardy's birthplace, Higher Bockhampton, is one of Dorset's most famous thatched cottages.

probably knock off the whole book in a single weekend but in doing so they would have missed the point and seen nothing. To fully appreciate the countryside it is necessary to go slowly with your eyes and ears open.

Some of the walks are short and level, ideal for a pipe opener on a winter's day, or giving plenty of time to dawdle away a summer's afternoon. Others are longer or more strenuous, some making an excellent all-day expedition. Certain of the walks involve some climbing. This is inevitable as hills add enormous interest to the countryside and with no hills there are no views. However, this presents no problem to the sensible walker who has three uphill gears — slowly, very slowly and admiring the view. None of the walks in this book are inherently hazardous but sensible care should be taken. Many of the falls that do happen are due to unsuitable footwear, particularly unridged soles since grass slopes can be as slippery as the more obviously hazardous wet, smooth rock. Proper walking shoes or boots also give some protection to the ankle. It is essential to look where you are putting your feet to avoid tripping up. Wainwright, the doyen of walkers in the Lake District, said that he never had a serious fall in all his years and thousands of miles of walking because he always looked where he put his feet and stopped if he wanted to admire the scenery.

All the routes are on public rights of way or permissive paths and have been carefully checked but, of course, in the countryside things do change; a gate is replaced by a stile or a wood is extended. Each walk is circular and is illustrated by a sketch map. An Ordnance Survey map is useful as well, especially for identifying the main features of views. The area is covered by Landranger 1:50 000 (1¼ inches to 1 mile) series, sheets 183, 193, 194, and 195. Even better for walking are the 1:25 000 Explorer maps 29, 117, 118 and 129 and Outdoor Leisure maps 15 and 22. The grid reference of the starting point and details of the appropriate maps are given for each walk.

In nearly every case, the walks are designed so that, starting where suggested, the teashop is reached in the second half so a really good appetite for tea can be worked up and then its effects walked off. Some walks start at a car park, which is ideal. Where this is not possible, the suggested starting place will always have somewhere a few cars can be left without endangering other traffic or causing inconvenience. However, it sometimes fits in better with the plans for the day to start and finish at the teashop and so for each walk there are details of how to do this.

Tea is often said to be the best meal to eat out in England and I believe that it is something to be enjoyed on all possible occasions. Scones and clotted cream and strawberry jam, delicious home-made cakes, toasted teacakes dripping with butter in winter, delicate cucumber sandwiches in summer, all washed down with the cup that cheers.

Dorset is particularly attractive to walkers who love their tea! In particular, it is far enough west for clotted cream to be readily available — the richest, most fattening and most wickedly delicious ambrosia. The best clotted cream is made from the milk of cows which have grazed lush pasture. It is heated gently for a long period of time so the cream forms a crust on top which is skimmed off. Bad for the figure maybe, but the walking will see to that.

The best teashops serve a range of cakes, all home-made and including fruit cake as well as scones and other temptations. Teapots should be capacious and pour properly. Most of the teashops visited on these walks fulfil these criteria admirably and they all offer a good tea. They always have at least light lunches available as well so there is no need to think of these walks as just something for the afternoons.

The pleasures of summer walking are obvious. Many of the teashops featured in this book have an attractive garden where tea can be taken outside when the weather is suitable. However, let me urge you not to overlook the pleasures of a good walk in winter. The roads and paths are quieter and what could be better than sitting by an open fire in a cosy teashop scoffing crumpets that you can enjoy with a clear conscience due to the brisk walk to get them!

There is an abundance of excellent establishments but, even so, teashops are not scattered evenly throughout the county. In some places popular with tourists, the visitor is spoilt for choice. In such cases the most convenient teashop that, in the author's opinion, most closely fulfils the criteria set out above is recommended but, should that not appeal, there are others from which to choose. In other places where there is a delightful walk to be enjoyed, the choice for tea may be more limited. However, they all offer a good tea partway round an attractive walk. The opening times and telephone number of each teashop are given. Some are rather vague about when they open out of season: it seems to depend on weather and mood. If you are planning a walk on a wet November Tuesday, for example, a call to check that tea will actually be available that day is a wise precaution. A few are definitely closed in the depths of winter and for these walks an alternative source of refreshment is given. In most cases, these are pubs serving food, which in some cases includes tea.

So put on your walking shoes and prepare to be delighted by the charms of Dorset and refreshed by a traditional English tea!

Jean Patefield

Walk 1
RINGWOOD FOREST

This walk, in the north-eastern tip of Dorset, is reminiscent of rambles in the nearby New Forest. The route is entirely within Ringwood Forest, which is planted woodland, but please don't let that deter you from this attractive walk as the forest is unusually open. The going is remarkably easy — all on well-made tracks and paths and mostly level — making this a suitable walk for times when other areas are unappealingly muddy underfoot. A charming miniature railway, perfect in every detail, has been built near the Visitor Centre. It will appeal to children and railway enthusiasts alike and the route described allows you to complete the leg before tea with a ride, if you wish. There is also an intriguing aerial path at tree-top height that can easily be included in the walk as a short diversion.

☕ The Visitor Centre for Moors Valley Country Park, containing a teashop, is housed in two 16th-century barns. There are tables outside in the shelter of the angle made by the buildings. A range of cakes is served, and an excellent selection of Danish pastries. For lunch the choice is wide, from full meals to snacks such as bacon sandwiches and pasties. Open every day throughout the year between 9.30 am and 4.30 pm, later in summer. Telephone: 01425 470537.

DISTANCE: 4 miles plus ½ mile for the optional tree top walk.

MAP: OS Landranger 195 Bournemouth and Purbeck or Outdoor Leisure 22 New Forest.

STARTING POINT: Small parking area for Ringwood Forest on the B3081 (GR 129057).

HOW TO GET THERE: From the A31 just west of Ringwood, take the B3081 towards Verwood to a parking area on the left immediately before a junction with a minor road to Alderholt.

ALTERNATIVE STARTING POINT: If you wish to visit the teashop at the beginning or end of your walk, start at Moors Valley Country Park Visitor Centre where there is ample parking (charge at most times of the year). The teashop is in the Visitor Centre. You will then start the walk at point 5.

THE WALK

1. Go to the rear of the parking area and follow the main track ahead to a cross track after 70 yards. Turn right for 200 yards then bear left at a fork. Follow this bridleway, marked by periodic blue arrows, for about a mile.

The Forestry Commission was set up in 1919 to create a strategic reserve of timber and concentrated upon conifers because they are very quick growing in the warm(!), wet British climate. The value of forests for recreation has been realised in more recent years as woods can absorb a lot of people without losing a sense of remoteness and this area was opened up as a country park in 1986. The forest also has abundant wildlife including the rare Dartford warbler and the tiny goldcrest. Open areas with warm, sandy soils are the favoured habitat of reptiles such as adders, slow worms and sand lizards but you are unlikely to see them — they are much more nervous of you than you could ever be of them and will hear your crashing boots approaching and slither away.

2. Turn right on a path marked by a green and yellow banded pole and signed 'Lookout'. Follow the path gently uphill to a pagoda-like structure with extensive views over the forest. After pausing to enjoy the view, continue on the main, waymarked path, soon swinging left

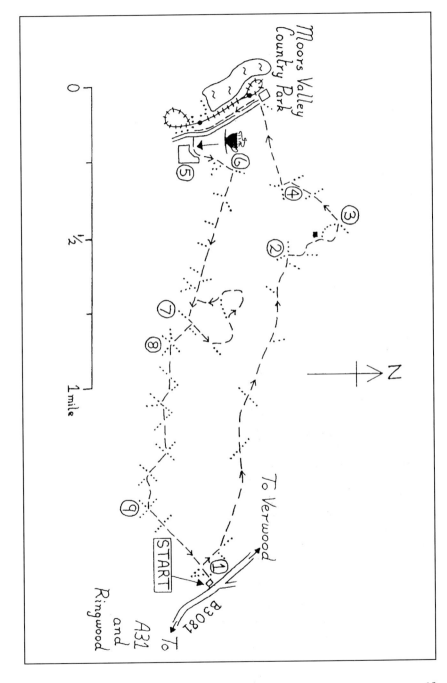

Steam up for a ride to tea.

and going downhill to a T-junction.

3. Turn left, signed 'Visitor Centre and Car Park', and follow the track to a T-junction immediately in front of a golf course.

4. Turn left for 50 yards then, at a four-way junction, take the first track on the right, between fences. Follow it across the golf course to the miniature railway station to catch a train. On disembarking cross the line then take the path beside the line to the Visitor Centre and tea, soon reached on the left. You have the choice of a short shuttle ride directly to Lakeside Station or a longer trip that goes round the children's play area first.
(If you do not wish to ride this short section, take the path between the railway and road to the Visitor Centre.)

The railway was moved here in 1985 and the station at Kingsmere, where you embark, was converted from a cowshed. It has a small buffet if you cannot wait for your tea! There are 12 steam engines, all fuelled by coal, and 30 carriages. The lake is man-made, the spoil being used to landscape the golf course. Trains run every day from Easter to mid-September, during local schools' half terms, during the Christmas holidays after Boxing Day and at the weekend in winter. The service operates from 10.45 am until 5 pm (telephone: 01425 470721).

5. From the Visitor Centre turn left and immediately left again by the cycle hire depot. Walk along this track, signed 'Lookout Tree Top Trail', for about 300 yards to a track on the right with a similar sign.

6. Turn right and follow the track for about ½ mile, ignoring several paths to both left and right. Pass a path on the left with 'no entry' signs and continue ahead to a T-junction and seat.

7. Turn left, signed 'Tree Top Trail', for 30 yards(*). Turn right again on an unsigned path as far as a six-way junction.
(*) An interesting diversion at this point is to continue ahead as far as the first track on the left. Turn left and this soon leads to an aerial footpath at canopy level. When this ends, continue ahead along this one-way path to rejoin the route at the 'no entry' signs passed earlier.

8. Take the second on the left, marked by a red banded post. Turn right at a T-junction, indicated by a red banded post, and after 90 yards, when the track forks, bear left for 20 yards. Now bear right on a smaller path, still guided by red waymarks. At the next complex junction, bear right on the main path and then at a five-way junction, follow the path round to the left, all the while following the route shown by the red banded posts. Continue to a T-junction with a major track.

9. Turn left. At the next major cross track the red banded route turns left, but we carry on ahead to rejoin the outward route 70 yards from the starting point.

Walk 2
PAMPHILL

In its short distance this easy walk displays all that is most appealing about pastoral southern England. It starts with a walk by the sparkling river Stour as it wends its way through meadows before an ancient, sunken path takes the route up to the attractive hamlet of Pamphill, complete with chocolate box cottages and tree-fringed village green, overlooked by a thatched cricket pavilion. Our enjoyment of this idyllic scene is enhanced by lunch or tea at a farm before an easy, downhill stroll back to the start.

Pamphill Parlour Restaurant at Pamphill Farm Shop specialises in home-cooked farmhouse fare. It is housed in what was once a dairy building — calf boxes stood where the teashop is now. The change was made in 1983 when milk quotas were introduced and the establishment has been going strong ever since. A good range of cakes is served, some a bit out of the ordinary, such as a delicious apricot and almond cake when I visited. Options at lunchtime include sandwiches and other snacks as well as full meals, including Sunday lunch. Open every day throughout the year except the week after Christmas. Telephone: 01292 880618.

DISTANCE: 3 miles.

MAP: OS Landranger 195 Bournemouth and Purbeck or Explorer 118 Shaftesbury and Cranborne Chase

STARTING POINT: Eyebridge car park (GR 995001).

HOW TO GET THERE: From the A31 at the Lake Gates roundabout, take the B3078 to Wimborne. At the Pudding and Pye turn left to continue along the B3078, signed 'Cranborne', for about ¼ mile. Turn left down Cowgrove Road for about ½ mile to a car park on the left. This is not signed from the road: it is just after Vine Hill on the right and Greenways Cottage on the left.

ALTERNATIVE STARTING POINT: If you wish to visit the teashop at the beginning or end of your walk, start in Pamphill where there is ample parking in two car parks. Walk along the lane towards the church and turn right. The teashop is on the left. You will then start the walk at point 6.

THE WALK

The Romans were here. A road crossed the river Stour at this point and there was a large fort at Lake, to the south, one of several built after the Second Augustan Legion subdued this part of England. Their commander, Vespasian, was later to become Emperor.

1. With your back to the lane and facing the river, turn right on a National Trust permissive path along the river bank.

2. On entering a wood, turn right on a path just within the wood, soon passing a magnificent, ancient oak on the right. Follow the path through the wood, then between fields and finally along the right-hand side of a field to emerge on a lane opposite Poplar Farm.

3. Cross the lane and turn left in front of the farm on a track, which soon passes to the right of a large pond.

4. As it reaches a lane, turn right on a track signed 'All Fools Lane'.

This is an ancient route, as we know from the way it is deeply eroded. There are badger sets in the banks. It crosses the line of the Roman road, mentioned earlier, though there is nothing to be seen.

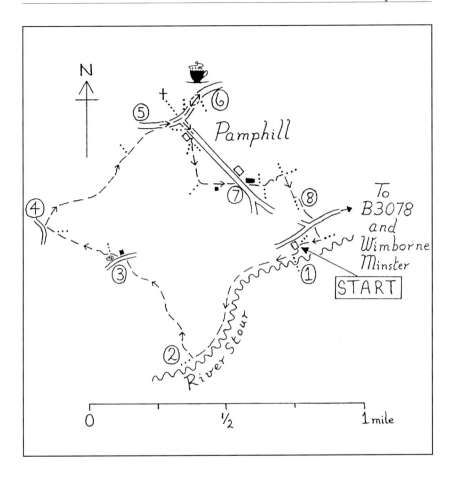

5. At a lane turn right, signed 'Stour Valley Way Pamphill ½'. Continue past the entrance to St Stephen's church to the teashop on the left.

Pamphill is a charming village with many 17th and 18th-century thatched cottages. It was the estate village for Kingston Lacey, Dorset's grandest house set in a lovely park. The house was built between 1631 and 1665 after the destruction of the Bankes' previous home at Corfe Castle (see walk 5). It was bequeathed to the National Trust in 1981 and is now open to the public, though not accessible from Pamphill. St Stephen's church, often locked, is a relatively modern building constructed in 1907 in Arts and Crafts Gothic style.

The attractive cricket pavilion at Pamphill.

6. Return to the entrance to the church and turn left along the lane opposite. Turn right on a track at the far end of a car park on the right. After 10 yards turn left on a path, bearing right at a fork after a further 10 yards to head round the right-hand side of the green, passing in front of the thatched cricket pavilion to return to the lane.

The school and almshouses date from the end of the 17th century — see the plaque over the door. Originally, the schoolmaster's quarters and the school room were in the centre with four single-roomed almshouses on each side. The school took over the whole building in 1971.

7. Turn right for a few yards to a school building on the left. Cross the green in front of the school to pick up a path, which soon passes beneath a monstrosity of a pylon. Follow the path downhill. Near the bottom of the hill, turn right on a cross path. Follow the main path when it turns left at a stile and goes down a few steps to soon reach another stile into a field.

Power lines and their supporting pylons marching across the countryside are never attractive. Power distribution cables can be buried underground, of course, but this is vastly more expensive than lines and pylons and is therefore only done in exceptional areas, such as National Parks.

8. Turn right, signed 'Stour Valley Way Wimborne', and walk along the right-hand side of the field to a stile onto a lane. Turn right for 20 yards then across a stile on the left. Follow the path ahead to the river bank and turn right, back to the start.

Walk 3
AGGLESTONE ROCK AND STUDLAND

*T*he outward and return legs of this outstanding walk are a complete contrast. The route before tea is across some of the best heathland remaining in southern England and the views from Agglestone Rock and Black Down are exceptional. There is a sense of altitude and remoteness that far exceeds the modest efforts needed to reach these spots. After tea at Studland, the shorter return leg is by the popular Studland Bay, lively with visitors in summer. On a clear day in August when the heather is in bloom, this walk is a memorable experience but it is enjoyable and highly recommended at all times.

Looking out for visitors to the tearoom.

Manor Farm Tearoom in Studland is a traditional farm teashop in a converted stable with some tables outside in the yard. The service is cheerful and friendly and there is a good selection of cakes temptingly displayed. Light lunches include sandwiches, quiche and ploughman's or, for a cooler day, soup with crusty bread. Open every day from Easter to the end of September and maybe weekends in October, depending on the weather, between 11.45 am and 5.30 pm. Telephone: 01929 450538.

When the teashop is closed, the Bankes Arms in Studland serves food.

DISTANCE: 4 miles.

MAP: OS Landranger 195 Bournemouth and Purbeck or Outdoor Leisure 15 Purbeck and South Dorset.

STARTING POINT: The National Trust car park at Knoll Beach, for which there is a charge (GR 034835).

HOW TO GET THERE: Take the B3351 from Corfe Castle to Studland and continue, signed 'Knoll Beach Car Park Bournemouth via Toll Ferry', to a car park on the right.

ALTERNATIVE STARTING POINT: It is not easy to visit the teashop at the beginning or end of your walk unless you can arrange to leave your car at the teashop car park. You will then start the walk at point 10.

THE WALK

1. Return to the car park entrance and turn left beside the road for about ¼ mile.

Ahead and to the left you can see Handfast Point with several detached chalk stacks called Old Harry Rocks. The Point is the seaward end of the ridge of chalk running across Purbeck and it is more resistant to erosion than the softer clays and sandstones around it. However, nothing resists the power of the sea forever; any weakness in the chalk is opened up and eroded into caves and arches. When the roof collapses an isolated stack is left, only to be further attacked by the waves and ultimately broken down. Erosion is still going on. Old Harry's wife collapsed in 1896 and local fishermen painted a black mourning band around Old Harry. The gap separating the largest stack, No Man's Land, was formed in 1921. A ship carrying a load of bells for Poole church foundered here as punishment, it is said, for the crew's blasphemy and ghostly bells are supposed to be heard pealing in wild weather.

2. Go through a small wooden gate on the right, signed 'Bridleway' and marked by a blue arrow. When the path fades out in a field, bear half left to a gap in the hedge.

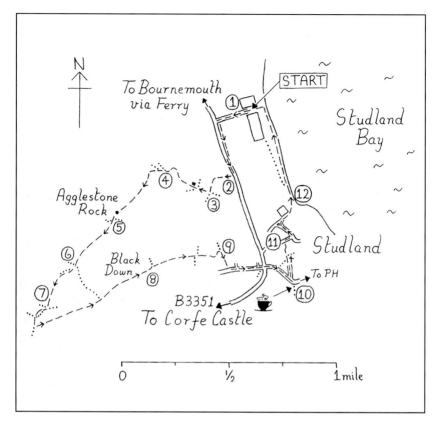

3. Turn right along a track. Bear right when it forks at Wadmore Farm, signed 'Agglestone Rock', and follow the sometimes muddy track through woodland and onto heath, Agglestone Rock coming into view.

4. Soon after emerging onto the heath, turn left off the bridleway onto a footpath on the left. Bear left at a fork and follow the path to Agglestone Rock.

The views of the surrounding heathland and across Poole Harbour are quite magnificent. Agglestone Rock is supposed to have been hurled at Corfe Castle by Satan who missed despite presumably demonic powers. It is a mass of hard, iron-rich sandstone that has resisted erosion more than the surrounding rock. It used to be perched on a narrow base but finally the forces of nature took their toll and it collapsed in 1970. It is about 18 feet high, 80 feet in diameter and weighs some 500

Agglestone Rock.

tons. *It is hard to believe that a terrible fire in 1986 burned the heath in a swathe round the rock and up to 1¹/₂ miles beyond so that only a gorse bush and a holly were left. The recovery has been remarkable.*

5. Take the path on the far side of the rock and follow it uphill, ignoring paths on the left and right.

Without the actions of man, the heathland would not exist. It originated when early farmers cleared the primeval forest and created an impoverished soil, deficient in many nutrients. Heathland plants such as heather, bog asphodel and the carnivorous sundews can thrive in these conditions. In the last couple of hundred years over 85% of lowland heath has disappeared, destroyed by the myriad pressures on the countryside. From this path, three of these are clearly visible — the golf course ahead, the dark green forestry plantations to the right and modern, intensive agriculture all around. All the remaining heaths are designated Sites of Special Scientific Interest and many, including this one, are carefully managed by bodies such as English Nature and the National Trust.

6. At a cross track continue ahead through a gate, now walking beside a golf course.

7. At a cross track turn right, ignoring an immediate smaller path on the right. Bear right at a fork after 30 yards then ignore a path on the right, signed 'Rempstone Forest', and continue on the main path, signed 'Studland Road ¼'. After a further 100 yards turn left, signed 'Studland Village 1¼'. Follow this path for a good ½ mile.

8. When the main path bears left, continue in the same direction over a stile, marked with a yellow arrow, to shortly join an unmade road. When this bends right, continue ahead through a gate and over a stile to a T-junction with a wider path.

9. Turn right to a road. Turn left. Continue ahead across a main road, along School Lane to the teashop on the right.

Studland has been through many metamorphoses in its long history. In the Domesday Book it is recorded as having 32 salt pits, an important commodity before the days of refrigeration. It was also a home to pirates in the 16th century and a notorious smuggling centre, the contraband being hidden in the seaweed collected from the beach to use as fertiliser. Note the village cross on the left just before the teashop. The new shaft was carved in 1976, combining traditional style with a modern theme.

10. Return along School Lane for a few yards then bear right along Church Road, signed 'Church only'. Continue ahead along a path to the left of the church to a lane.

St Nicholas' church is reputedly the oldest intact building in Dorset and is a fine example of early Norman architecture. There has been an important building on this site since pre-Christian times. During excavations in the 1880s, three layers of burials were found: modern ones on top, Saxon ones in the middle and pre-Christian graves beneath. There was certainly a church here 1,300 years ago and traces of the Saxon masonry are found in the north and south walls. Have a look at the corbel table at the junction of the walls and roof outside. It is decorated with grotesque carvings, some of them rather rude. The gravestone of Sergeant William Lawrence to the south-west of the porch gives great detail about his illustrious military career in the 40th Regiment of Foot. He fought at Waterloo then married a French girl, Clotilde, and came to Studland where he lived for another 54 years as a pub landlord. When he died his hope for a military style funeral was respected, and volunteers fired a volley over his grave.

11. Turn right and then left at a T-junction. (Turn right for the Bankes Arms). At the next T-junction turn right and go downhill to the right of Middle Beach car park to the shore.

Enid Blyton used to enjoy holidays at Studland. PC Plod from the Noddy books is said to be based on the local bobby she spotted on his beat round these lanes.

12. Turn left along the beach or on the path behind the dunes, back to the start.

Walk 4
WORTH MATRAVERS

This easy walk starts by going down to the cliff top behind Langton Matravers at the famous Dancing Ledge. There is then a stretch of idyllic cliff top walking on short, springy turf before a gentle climb to the attractive village of Worth Matravers, complete with duck pond and teashop. The return uses an ancient, level footpath with excellent views, initially over the sea and then to nearby Swanage with the Isle of Wight beyond.

☕ Worth Tea Shop is an attractive traditional tearoom overlooking the village green and duck pond. It has tables in its well-maintained garden, some under cover. Clotted cream teas are served with jam or local honey and a good selection of cakes is offered. For lunch, possibilities range from sandwiches through salads and omelettes to full meals such as trout and almonds or cottage pie. Open every day from Easter to mid October between 11 am and 5.30 pm. In winter it opens at the weekends, perhaps closing a little earlier. Telephone: 01929 439368.

When the teashop is closed, the pub in Worth Matravers, the Square and Compass, named after the stonemason's tools, serves food.

DISTANCE: 5 miles.

MAP: OS Landranger 195 Bournemouth and Purbeck or Outdoor Leisure 15 Purbeck and South Dorset.

STARTING POINT: Spyway Farm parking area (GR 997783).

HOW TO GET THERE: At Langton Matravers on the B3069, near the junction with the A351 west of Swanage, take a minor road called Durnford Drove, signed 'Langton House'. Follow this until it becomes an unsurfaced track that shortly leads to a grassy parking area on the right.

ALTERNATIVE STARTING POINT: If you wish to visit the teashop at the beginning or end of your walk, start in Worth Matravers where some street parking may be possible. The teashop is in the centre of the village overlooking the duck pond. You will then start the walk at point 5.

THE WALK

1. Continue along the track, going over a cross track. Pass between farm buildings and carry on in the same direction across two fields then down a steep path, signed 'Dancing Ledge'.

Spyway Farm belongs to the National Trust. The Great Barn is more than 200 years old and was completely renovated in 1993. Some of the dry-stone walls in this area were constructed by Napoleonic prisoners of war.

Dancing Ledge was made by quarrymen to win the valuable Purbeck marble. It is famous for its puffin colony, now greatly reduced. Some 50 years ago, hundreds of pairs were present and sadly today there are fewer than 10 pairs of these attractive birds whose white cheeks and colourful, parrot-like bills give them a rather comical appearance. They nest in clefts and are best seen in spring, flying in and out of the west cliff.

2. Turn right along the cliff path, signed 'Seacombe 1'. At the first valley, Seacombe Bottom, the path turns inland for a short distance behind an old quarry. Do not continue on the path up the valley bottom but turn left up some steps, signed 'Winspit $3/4$', to continue along the coast path to Winspit Bottom.

This coast is riddled with disused quarries that used to produce great quantities of Purbeck marble. This isn't really marble but a type of limestone that will take a

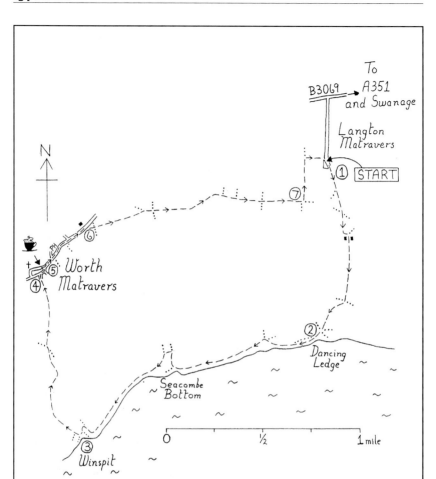

polish and has been used for decorative work since Roman times. The stone from these coastal quarries was loaded onto boats and ferried round to Swanage for export. Seacombe once produced a stone trough for the North Woolwich Galvanising Company that weighed 3½ tons and was 8 feet long, 4 feet wide and 4 feet deep. The quarrying ceased from the 1930s onwards.

This is a dangerous coast and many ships have come to grief. At two o'clock in the morning on 6 January 1786 the 758 ton East Indiaman, the 'Halsewell', foundered in a blizzard. The captain and 167 others were lost, including two of the captain's daughters and two nieces. Some of the victims are buried in the *churchyard at Worth Matravers. A mirror, reputed to come from the Halsewell, hangs in the vestry of the church.*

3. Turn right, signed 'Worth 1¼'. Bear right at a fork, signed 'Worth ½', and follow the path up to the village.

4. At a road turn right. Turn right at a junction then left across the village green, past the pond, to the teashop.

Everything in Worth Matravers is built of Purbeck stone from the 12th-century church to the duck pond, giving the village an architectural homogeneity, which contributes much to its attractive appearance. The village was home to one of the unsung pioneers of medicine. Benjamin Jesty noticed that dairymaids and cowmen rarely caught smallpox and learned that they had usually suffered from cowpox, a much milder ailment. In 1774, more than 20 years before Jenner's famous experiments, he deliberately infected his wife and sons with cowpox, using a knitting needle. Their trust in him is impressive and fortunately the experiment was a success; Elizabeth Jesty outlived her husband and reached the grand age of 84. In 1805 he was invited to London to give evidence before the Vaccine Pock Institution. The doctors were so impressed with his pioneering spirit, they had his portrait painted as a mark of respect.

5. From the teashop turn left along the road, bearing right at a junction by the Square and Compass, and walk out of the village, ignoring a path on the right.

6. Immediately after a large barn on the left, take a path on the right, signed 'Swanage 4', and follow it across three fields to join a track. Press on in the same direction along the track for about a mile.

The resort of Swanage, seen ahead, was once a hamlet in the parish of Worth Matravers. This ancient path, called the Priest's Way, was the route taken by the cleric from Worth to take services in the chapel at Swanage.

7. Watch for a path on the right signed 'Dancing Ledge'. Do not take this path but some 25 yards further on take a path on the left, signed 'Langton ½ Toms Field'. Follow the path along the left-hand side of a field. At the end, turn right across the field to a stile onto a track and turn right to shortly reach the start.

Walk 5
CORFE CASTLE

The gaunt remains of Corfe Castle, reaching to the sky, are one of the enduring images of Dorset. They are in view for much of this remarkably varied route which encompasses fields, heath and woodland and has less climbing than other walks in this hilly corner of the county. The approach to Corfe Castle is along a hillside with one of the best displays of spring flowers, including bluebells, celandines and primroses, it has ever been my privilege to enjoy. The climax is tea under the ramparts of the castle followed by an easy stroll back to the start or, if you prefer, a five minute ride by steam train.

 The National Trust tearoom at Corfe Castle is a traditional beamed establishment and has several tables in the garden by the castle walls. It serves a good selection of delicious cakes as well as set teas, such as gardener's tea with a cheese scone, and cream teas. Possibilities for lunch range from sandwiches through filled jacket potatoes to a daily hot special. A farmer's lunch with various options including Dorset Blue Vinney cheese or ham is a tempting suggestion. Open throughout the year from 10 am until 5.30 pm between March and October, closing at 4 pm in the winter months. Telephone: 01929 481332.

DISTANCE: 5 miles.

MAP: OS Landranger 195 Bournemouth and Purbeck or Outdoor Leisure 15 Purbeck and South Dorset.

STARTING POINT: Norden park and ride car park. Ideally, park at the far end of the second parking area (GR 958828).

HOW TO GET THERE: The car park where the walk starts is signed from the A351, Swanage to Wareham road, at a roundabout just north of Corfe Castle.

ALTERNATIVE STARTING POINT: If you wish to visit the teashop at the beginning or end of your walk, start in Corfe Castle where there is some parking in signed car parks. The teashop is in The Square by the entrance to the castle. You will then start the walk at point 15.

THE WALK

1. Go to the far end of the car park and leave through a wooden kissing gate. Turn left, signed 'Scotland ½'. The sign is not wrong by several hundred miles but refers to a farm passed on the route! Shortly cross a road and continue up some steps on the other side and across a field to a wood. Follow the path through the wood then in the next field bear right to head for a stile 25 yards to the left of the far right corner. (Note: if the path is impassable due to crops, skirt round the right perimeter of this large field.)

2. Continue on the waymarked path, bearing right at a fork and soon crossing heathery heath where there is a maze of small paths. Press on in the same direction to a board walk over a marshy area and cross this to a lane.

Lowland heath is a man-made habitat created when the native forest was cleared by early farmers. Nonetheless, it supports a diverse and important wildlife community. It is one of the habitats most under threat from the pressures of the modern world and over four fifths have been lost in the last 200 years. Attempts are being made in this area to regenerate it. This involves reducing the fertility of the soil as the heathland vegetation thrives on impoverished soil. Perversely, nitrogen fertiliser is first applied. This encourages grass to grow and consume the other

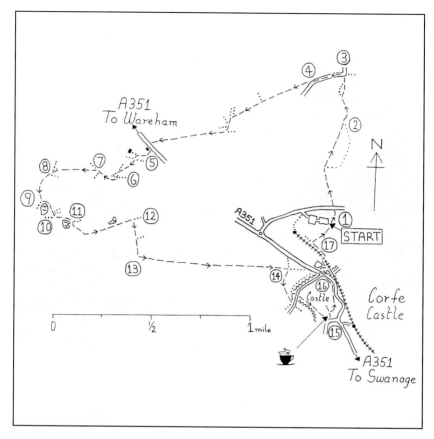

nutrients in the soil. The grass is then cut and removed, taking with it the nutrients it contains. Sometimes local heather seed is spread but ploughing also can help the heather to get a foothold again: heather seed can remain viable in the soil for up to 50 years and ploughing brings it to the surface where it germinates.

3. Turn left.

The views to the left show the superb defensive position of Corfe Castle. The gap in the chalk ridge dividing Purbeck from the rest of the county was eroded by streams which rise in the Purbeck Hills and flow north to Poole Harbour as Corfe River. A smaller hillock was left in the gap and this has been used as the base of the castle. There was a royal building here before the Conquest and tradition has it that this is where young King Edward was murdered by his stepmother, Queen Elfrida, ambitious for her own son, Ethelred, famously Unready. The story goes that in

The tea room garden at Corfe Castle.

AD 978 the young king was hunting in Purbeck and called in for refreshment. Whilst he was drinking a cup of wine, still seated on his horse, one of the queen's servants stabbed him in the back. He galloped off but fainted in the saddle and was dragged by the stirrup to a place on the Wareham road since called St Edward's cottage. The body was buried at Wareham and later reburied at Shaftesbury. He was canonised and many strange and miraculous happenings were reported. For example, his body is said to have been originally put down a well. It emitted a shaft of light so that it could be found and thereafter, the well water had miraculous curative powers. The murderous Elfrida retired to a convent at Wherwell in Hampshire to lead a more virtuous life, apparently becoming Abbess. It is said that she tried to join the funeral procession as it left Wareham but that each horse she mounted refused to move.

4. When the lane bears left, continue in the same direction along a track. Follow this to a surfaced track. Turn left and walk along it to a main road.

5. Cross the road and take an unsurfaced track a few yards to the left at the side of a thatched cottage with a 1710 plaque. Just before the track ends at bungalows go over a stile on the left and follow the waymarked path, soon crossing a broad track, which is a section of the disused Swanage railway.

6. Immediately after a track joins from the right turn left on a path marked by a yellow arrow on a post. Soon cross another track and follow the possibly damp, meandering path through the woods to a gate giving onto heath.

7. Through the gate fork left, signed 'E Creech 1¼', on a path heading across heath towards a wood. As you approach the trees, bear left, following the arrows on short posts.

8. At a cross path in front of a wire fence turn left for about ¼ mile to a signed cross path.

You may be surprised to see such a fearsome fence in apparently rather wild countryside. This encloses the famous Blue Pool, a local beauty spot. Clay was dug from round here from the 17th century onwards when it was used for making tobacco pipes. The pits flooded, forming pools, of which the Blue Pool is one. The route passes several others.

9. Turn left, signed 'Norden Farm 1', and follow a narrow path to the left of the pool to a gate. Through the gate go ahead a few yards to a T-junction with a cross path.

10. Turn left, signed 'Norden Farm 1'.

11. Immediately after passing a pool on the right, turn right over a wooden bridge and follow the path through the wood. At the edge of the wood bear left to walk just inside it for about ¼ mile.

12. Turn right on a path signed 'Corfe 1½'. Walk along the right-hand side of two fields and up the left-hand side of a third to a stile.

13. Over the stile, pause to admire the extensive views then turn left for about ¾ mile. Cross a stile and go ahead to a second stile.

The bank on the right is a mass of primroses, bluebells, celandines and archangels

*in late spring. Later in the year, bracken, overwintering as rhizomes in the soil,
springs up but the essentially woodland flowers will return next year to delight us
again.*

14. Do not cross the second stile but turn right on a cross path
and follow this round the hill to a stile. Over the stile, turn left then
right, signed 'Village Centre The Castle'. Cross a river and a lane and
continue on a surfaced path to Corfe Castle and the teashop on
the left.

*The little town of Corfe grew up round the skirts of the great castle. It was
particularly prosperous from the 12th to 14th centuries due to the stone trade.
Purbeck marble is a type of limestone which will polish up and was greatly in
demand. Great quantities of stone were exported from the quarries to the south
through Corfe and dragged north across the heath to be sent by ship from Ower and
other ports round Poole Harbour. The right of way to Ower was kept open by a game
of football. A ball, supplied by the most recently married man, was kicked from
Corfe to Ower Farm and presented with a pound of pepper, before continuing onto
the quay. Men called de Corfe worked on churches throughout Europe. The trade
declined but buildings continued to be constructed of local stone, which gives the
town a satisfying homogeneity.*

15. Turn left beside the teashop as though going to the castle and
cross the moat. Immediately before an arch into the castle grounds,
turn right under the ramparts to shortly join the main road.

*Work on the castle was started in the 1080s and several kings contributed to its
construction. It was King John's favourite castle and he paid £1,400 for walls, a
ditch and bank and a 'gloriette', an unfortified residence within the grounds. He
also used it as a prison. Having disposed of his nephew, Arthur of Brittany, he
imprisoned 24 of his knights who had fought for Arthur and starved 22 of them to
death. He also kept Arthur's sister, Eleanor, prisoner here as well as Isabel and
Margery, daughters of the King of Scotland. The castle passed out of royal hands in
the time of Elizabeth I and eventually came into the ownership of the Bankes family.
They were ardent Royalists and Corfe Castle was for a time the only Royalist
stronghold between London and Exeter. The defence was organised by Lady Bankes
and it only fell to the Parliamentarians by deception or betrayal. Some claim that a
member of the garrison turned traitor and admitted the besieging soldiers whereas
others say that a small group of soldiers got into the castle by pretending to be
Royalists and then opened the gates to the rest. Whatever the truth, the castle was
subjected to an unusually brutal slighting by gunpowder and undermining to leave*

the splendid ruin we see today. The castle is in the care of the National Trust and is open every day (charge; free to NT members). Telephone: 01929 481294.

If you wish to return to the start by train, turn left into The Square on leaving the teashop and cross over to Station Road to the right of the Bankes Arms. The station lies along this on the left.

The railway to Swanage closed in 1972 but it is being brought back to life by the Swanage Railway Company. Trains presently run as far as Norden, just north of Corfe and the starting point of this walk, and it is hoped they will eventually go all the way to Wareham. The timetable varies with the seasons. Information: 01929 425800.

16. Turn left to the car park for the castle where there is an informative exhibition. Go to the back right corner of the car park to pick up a path initially by the railway line and then across it. Over the line, turn left, signed 'Park and ride ³/₄ Scotland 1¹/₂', to continue in the same direction for about 300 yards.

17. Turn right, signed 'Park and ride ¹/₂ Scotland 1', and follow the clear path back to the start.

Walk 6
KIMMERIDGE

*A*ll *the walks in Purbeck have excellent views, but this route beats the lot! The first leg is up to Swyre Head, the highest point in Purbeck, with a 360° panorama. The route then drops down to the coast path for a 1½ mile westwards cliff walk to Kimmeridge Bay with the spectacular cliffs of Worbarrow ahead of you all the way. This is followed by a climb back up Smedmore Hill for the climax of the circuit — the mile long ridge walk with the sea on one hand and the rolling Dorset countryside stretching into the blue yonder on the other. Such rich rewards are not gained without some effort. The path from Swyre Head down to the coast at Rope Lake Head is very steep to begin with and should not be attempted without suitable footwear. The climb back to the ridge is also steep and long but a good tea at Kimmeridge and the promise of the delights to come should give you the energy to tackle it.*

☕ KBay Restaurant is housed in an attractive thatched building originally constructed as the village school. It also contains the village shop and post office. In winter there is a wood-burning stove inside and in summer there are tables outside, some shaded from the sun under a pergola. The selection of cakes includes a delicious Dorset apple cake, served warm with clotted cream, and there are also the usual teatime temptations including cream teas. Lunchtime appetites are satisfied with full meals such as breaded pork stuffed with Stilton and children's portions are available. For a lighter option a variety of things on toast are offered, such as garlic fried tomatoes on toast, as well as the usual sandwiches and ploughman's. Open throughout the year from 9 am. Telephone: 01929 480701.

DISTANCE: 6 miles.

MAP: OS Landranger 195 Bournemouth and Purbeck or Outdoor Leisure 15 Purbeck and South Dorset.

STARTING POINT: Swyre Head car park (GR 943792).

HOW TO GET THERE: From the B3069 Corfe Castle to Langton Matravers road, turn into Kingston at the Scott Arms, along West Street. Follow this road through the village. Pass one car park just outside the village and continue for about a mile to a second on the left.

ALTERNATIVE STARTING POINT: Parking in the village of Kimmeridge is very restricted. There is a small car park by the teashop and there are two car parks just outside the village and passed on the route that could be used. If you wish to visit the teashop at the beginning of your walk, start at the car park at Kimmeridge Bay (charge). You will then start the walk at point 5. To visit the teashop at the end of your walk, start at a small car park in a disused quarry on the road to Kimmeridge at GR 918800. You will then start the walk at point 9.

THE WALK

1. Take the lane at the side of the car park, passing between stone pillars. After a few yards turn right on a track signed 'Swyre Head 1'. Follow the track to Swyre Head.

To your left as you walk along the track is an area known as the Golden Bowl, sheltering Encombe House — a fertile valley between the bare down and the wild coast. It was the home of John Scott, 1st Earl of Eldon, who was Lord Chancellor for 26 years in the 19th century, longer than any other person. Swyre Head at 666 feet is the highest point of Purbeck and has impressive views, especially west to Worbarrow Tout, sadly an army training area. The grassy mound on top is a tumulus.

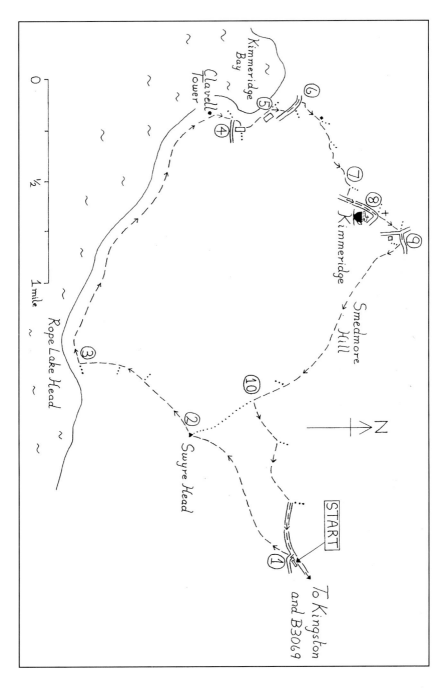

The Clavell monument.

2. Follow a path towards the coast, signed 'Permissive path to Rope Lake Head and coast path'. This descends very, very steeply to begin with but then levels out. Continue until you meet the coast path, ignoring tracks to right and left.

3. Turn right for about 1½ miles to Kimmeridge Bay.

The tower was built in 1831 by John Clavell as a garden feature for nearby Smedmore House, the seat of the Clavells. It was later used as a coastguard lookout. An earlier John Clavell, born in 1603, was the black sheep of the family. Despite his prosperous background as nephew to the man who built Smedmore, he became a highwayman, preying on travellers on Gad's Hill near Rochester. He was caught and condemned to the gallows in 1627 but managed to escape the noose. While in prison he wrote repentant poems, which so affected Queen Henrietta Maria that she begged his pardon from the king. His uncle was not so easily swayed and disinherited him. He died in 1642, aged 39.

4. Cross a lane and follow the path ahead round and up into a field used as a car park. Turn left and continue round the bay to the far end of a second parking area.

The geology of Kimmeridge Bay gives it a rather sombre feel with its cliffs of dark shale alternating with yellowish limestone bands. The rocks were laid down in Jurassic times, some 135 million years ago, under the sea. They contain many fossils but it is impossible to remove fossils intact from shale as it crumbles so easily, so don't even try — you will just be destroying something that has survived millions of years. The cliffs are dangerous. The shale layers are very soft and erode easily but are given some support by the harder limestone. Shale often falls from the cliffs and larger falls of limestone occur when the shale underneath has eroded.

It is difficult today to imagine this spot as a hive of industry but there have been various attempts to make use of the shale. In Roman times jet-like jewellery and even furniture was made because as long as the shale is kept oiled, it can be polished to a shine. If it dries out, it crumbles away. Later, it was quarried to make alum, an important chemical in tanning, printing and dyeing. The works were fuelled by shale, known as Kimmeridge coal, which gives off stinking, sulphurous fumes and oily smoke when burned. Later still, glass-making and extraction of chemicals, including gas for street lighting, were other initiatives. It was planned to use the gas extracted to light the streets of Paris but it was too smelly. Fortunately for the environment hereabouts, only the Romans had any commercial success. Oil is extracted today at the rate of 100,000 gallons a week by nodding donkey wells from reserves thousands of feet below ground and stored in discreet green tanks.

The ledges make wonderful places to study shore life because they have both vertical and horizontal surfaces. Kimmeridge Bay is part of the Purbeck Marine Wildlife Reserve and there is an information centre in one of the huts.

5. Turn right to a road. Turn left along the road for 150 yards to the **second** path on the right.

6. Turn right through a metal gate on a track along the right-hand side of a field to a gate and stile by a barn with a rusting metal roof. Over the stile, continue along the right-hand side of a second field as far as a stile on the right. Cross this and follow a path round the right-hand side of a third field until the path comes to two stiles, one on the right and one ahead, both leading to small bridges.

7. Go over the stile on the right into a field and cross over to a stile in the far left corner giving onto a road. Turn left into the village and the teashop is on the right.

Kimmeridge lies about a mile inland and is a small, charming village of thatched cottages. The church is essentially Norman but was heavily restored in the 19th century.

8. From the teashop turn right and continue up the road to the church. As the road bends right, carry on in the same direction through the churchyard and on steeply up a field to a stile giving onto the road at a junction.

9. Take a small lane opposite for about 100 yards then turn right on a track and continue uphill, ignoring an immediate track on the right. The track soon reaches the ridge and there follows an outstanding section of the walk.

10. The track reaches two gates, one ahead and one on the left marked by an arrow, pink at the time of writing. Go through the gate on the left, heading towards the tower of Kingston church, and walk along the right-hand side of a field. At the end of the field, follow the track round to the right and continue ahead when it becomes a surfaced lane, ignoring the drive to Orchard Hill Farm on the left. This soon leads back to the start.

Walk 7
LULWORTH

This is a short walk but you will be able to enjoy a really good tea (as if you needed any justification!) as the route has two stiff climbs — one at the start and one after tea. As well as rewarding yourself with excellent cake or (and!) scones, you will enjoy outstanding views of some of England's best loved coastal scenery, well known for its particularly interesting geology. This means that the first section of the walk towards the unusual formation of Durdle Door is unlikely to be quiet, unless you choose to do this walk on a rainy Tuesday in November. Nonetheless, this is a superb route, not to be missed.

The Gallery in West Lulworth is a friendly establishment in an unpretentious building on the main street in the village. It has limited indoor accommodation and several tables outside on the patio, each with its own vase of flowers on my visit. The cream teas feature delicious scones made to Great-aunt Lily's recipe and there is also a good selection of cakes and pastries. For lunch, a wide range of sandwiches and filled baguettes or jacket potatoes are available. The Gallery is open from 9 am every day between Easter and the end of October and at weekends in winter, when more hot food is included on the menu. Telephone: 01929 400417.

When the teashop is closed, there are cafés and hotels at Lulworth Cove that serve food.

DISTANCE: 3 miles.

MAP: OS Landranger 194 Dorchester, Weymouth and surrounding area or Outdoor Leisure 15 Purbeck and South Dorset.

STARTING POINT: Lulworth Cove car park, for which there is a charge (GR 821801).

HOW TO GET THERE: From the A352 Dorchester to Wareham road or the B3071 from Wool, take the B3070 through West Lulworth to the car park at Lulworth Cove.

ALTERNATIVE STARTING POINT: Parking in West Lulworth, where the teashop is situated, is very restricted and not recommended. For refreshment at the start or end of this walk, visit one of the establishments near the car park.

THE WALK

Before starting the walk, it is worth going to view the interesting geology. Go to the bottom of the car park, turn right on a minor road opposite Lulworth Cove Hotel and then bear left on a path signed 'Stair Hole'. Retrace your steps to the car park.

Lulworth Cove is not only a beauty spot, it is a textbook example of the effect of the sea on rocks of differing hardness and what happens to rocks when continents move. Rocks spanning 127 million years of the Earth's history have been laid down, one on top of the next, spanning the rise and fall of the dinosaurs, and are magnificently exposed in the cliffs. The continents seem immutable to us but, taking a geological timespan, they are waltzing around the surface of the globe like a mobile, ill-fitting jigsaw. Some 70 million years ago, the plate on which Africa rides smashed into the plate to the north, crumpling the surface into folds and throwing up the Alps and the chalk hills of southern England. This is what contorted the strata from the horizontal position in which they were laid down to the vertical layers we can see at Stair Hole. The rocks nearest the sea are Purbeck limestone, which is quite resistant to erosion. However, in places the sea has broken through, eroding small arches underneath and getting to work on the softer chalk behind. This is another Lulworth Cove in the making and eventually, quite soon in geological time but not

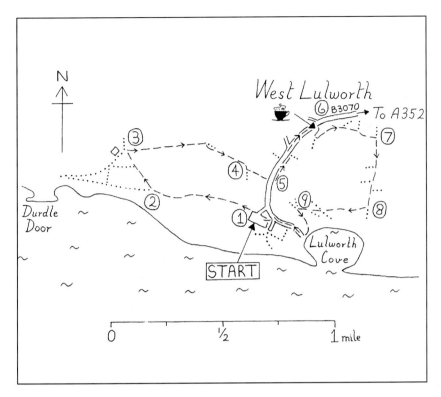

in our lifetime, the two will join. Thus, the features of our landscape are in constant evolution. The Heritage Centre in the car park has an informative display about several features of the natural and human history of this unusual place.

1. Standing in the car park, face its entrance and go to the left-hand side, then follow the clear, well-made path up the hillside.

2. At the top bear right on a less obvious path, signed 'Durdle Door coast path ½', towards a caravan site. The path leads over the hill to a stile and on to a second stile into a car park.

Turn left for better views of Durdle Door. Here the sea has eroded a great arch in the limestone through which the sea surges. Sometime in the future, the top of the arch will collapse, leaving a stack similar to Old Harry Rocks at Studland (see walk 3).

3. Do not go over the second stile but turn right and follow the path along the left-hand side of three fields. At the end of the third field go

Lulworth Cove.

over a stile a few yards to the right to continue on a path signed 'Lulworth Cove and Village'.

4. Go over a stile on the left to pick up a path signed 'West Lulworth Youth Hostel ¾', which goes down steps. At the bottom go over a stile and walk along the right-hand side of a field to a stile onto a road.

 5. Cross the road to a path beside it and turn left. When the path rejoins the road, continue ahead through the village to the teashop on the right.

West Lulworth shelters from the elements a mile inland. Walking into the village, you may have noticed that the church, unusually, is on the outskirts. Though extended in 1842 it was still too small for the needs of the parish and in a dilapidated condition, so it was pulled down and a new one built on a larger site at the end of the village.

6. From the teashop continue along the road for a few yards then turn right up some steps. Follow the path round to the right and when it forks, bear left on a path along the hillside above the village. Continue to a stile.

7. Over the stile, turn right uphill along the right-hand side of a field. Go over another stile and carry on uphill by a fence on the left then down the other side.

The top of Bindon Hill is occupied by a vast series of Iron Age earthworks enclosing an area of about 400 acres and, as you will see to your left, used by the British Army today for firing ranges. Paths across the ranges are sometimes open but the extensive Army use of this part of Dorset means we have limited enjoyment of a lovely part of England. It is said that the Army's activities are less disruptive to wildlife than farming and visitors so I suppose even the most annoying cloud has some silver lining. Two thousand years ago, the Roman army was here: they camped within the hill fort following their conquest of the local Veneti.

In 1832 a butterfly was discovered that only occurs in this part of Dorset. It is called the Lulworth Skipper and is one of the few British butterflies to have increased in number this century. The female has to find a tall specimen of Tor grass on which to lay her eggs. She walks backwards down the stem, laying up to 15 eggs as she goes. The first thing the caterpillar does when it hatches is to spin a cocoon in which it passes the winter. It emerges the following spring and feeds on the grass. When it is fully grown in June, it changes into a butterfly which can be seen on the wing until the weather cools down in September. It is estimated that 400,000 of this species live on Bindon Hill. During the 20th century there has been a reduction in sheep farming for economic reasons and in rabbit numbers due to myxomatosis. This has allowed the grass to grow taller so the butterfly population has increased.

8. Turn right immediately before a stile over a wire fence on a path signed 'Durdle Door 2 West Lulworth $^3/_4$'. Follow the path high above Lulworth Cove with excellent views across the cove until the fence on the left ends and a wall starts.

From this path you get an almost aerial view of the cove. As explained above, the sea has breached the harder, outer rock and is busily eating away the softer chalk so these cliffs are disappearing. Part of the Iron Age fort built on top of the hill has since been eroded. The shelter of the cove was attractive to smugglers and pirates. The traffic wasn't all one way. In the 16th century, horses, guns, grain and food were smuggled from England to France. Many excise men did a difficult job to the best of their ability, at risk to life and limb. In 1832, two Lulworth coastguards were attacked with flails on the cliffs. One was left for dead. The other, Thomas Knight, was thrown from the cliffs to his death; it was his forty-second birthday. Others were less dedicated and were friends of or related to the smugglers.

9. Turn left over a stile and follow a path downhill to the cove. Turn right along a lane, back to the car park.

John Keats spent his final hours in England here in September 1820 when his ship put in whilst waiting for a favourable wind to continue her journey to Italy. He is said to have written his last sonnet, 'Bright Star, would I were steadfast as thou art', whilst ashore.

Walk 8
FONTMELL DOWN AND
COMPTON ABBAS

There may be better downland walks than this, but not many! The carpet of wildflowers in summer and the magnificent views at any time of the year will refresh your spirit while tea at an excellent traditional teashop will similarly re-energize your body after the modest exertion needed to enjoy these delights. The return to the start is easy, along a road and field paths. Please note that a couple of stretches are likely to be muddy, so wear footwear that will keep you dry shod.

Milestones at Compton Abbas is to be found in a 17th-century building. It was used as a retreat house in the 1950s and the tearoom was then the chapel. Today it offers bodily rather than spiritual sustenance including a good selection of delicious cakes. The excellent Dorset apple cake may be enjoyed warm with clotted cream. A variety of set teas are offered such as cream teas and a farmhouse tea with a boiled egg. For a light lunch, home-made quiche, sandwiches and jacket potatoes with various fillings are available. As well as the tearoom, there is a pleasant conservatory and tables outside overlooking the well-tended garden. Milestones is open daily, except Thursdays, between 10 am and 5.30 pm from Easter until November. Telephone: 01747 811360.

When the teashop is closed, the Crown in Fontmell Magna serves food.

DISTANCE: 4½ miles.

MAP: OS Landranger 183 Yeovil and Frome or Explorer 118 Shaftesbury and Cranborne Chase.

STARTING POINT: Outskirts of Fontmell Magna (GR 868168).

HOW TO GET THERE: From the A350 Shaftesbury to Blandford Forum road, 4½ miles south of Shaftesbury, at Fontmell Magna, turn on a minor road signed 'Ashmore'. Park in one of the pull-offs on the right, being careful not to cause inconvenience for the houses. Should these pull-offs be full, you should be able to find a spot to park in Fontmell Magna.

ALTERNATIVE STARTING POINT: If you wish to visit the teashop at the beginning or end of your walk, start in Compton Abbas where there are a few parking spots by the church. The teashop is 50 yards along the road towards Fontmell Magna. You will then start the walk at point 9, turning right out of the teashop, first right and right at a T-junction.

THE WALK

1. Continue along the lane, passing some attractive ponds on the right, well supplied with ducks and ducklings in season.

Fontmell comes from the Old English for spring, funta, and the Celtic for bare hill, mael. The stream rises here, at Springhead, where there has been a mill since the time of the Domesday Book. Today it consists of a fine thatched house with the mill building at right angles to it backed by beautiful gardens, occasionally open to the public. Springhead was bought in 1933 by Rolf Gardiner who promoted summer music schools until his death in 1973. The Springhead Trust continues his work.

2. Just after Springhead Farm on the left, as the road swings right, continue in the same direction on a fenced track. The track ends at a gate across it with a stile beside. Continue ahead to a second gate, entering Fontmell Down Nature Reserve, and then carry on uphill, sticking to the main path.

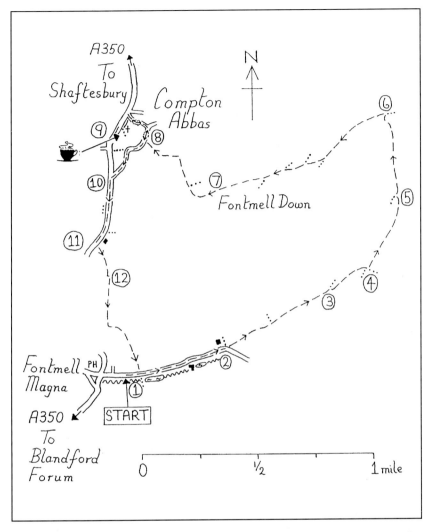

If you look at the vegetation around your feet you will see that it is not just grass but a rich variety of short herbs. In summer when they are in bloom, the sight is a delight. This typical downland ecosystem results from grazing by rabbits and sheep and, without the nibbling animals, it would quickly revert to scrub and then woods. The animals' teeth nip off any tender, germinating trees or shrubs and prevent them becoming established. There has been a substantial decline in chalk grassland in recent decades. Much has been ploughed up on gentler gradients. On steeper slopes, the threat is from changed economics of farming making sheep rearing less

attractive and from smaller rabbit populations due to myxomatosis. Therefore, in a nature reserve, if the managers just sit back and let nature get on with it, that which they wish to preserve will soon disappear. Management, in the form of controlled grazing and weeding out of scrub, is essential. The management regime here varies slightly from place to place to maintain as much diversity as possible.

3. Just below the top of the field the path makes a T-junction with a larger path. Turn right to reach a stile by a gate after 20 yards. Through the gate, continue, now more gently uphill through woods to a cross track.

4. Turn left.

5. Some 90 yards after passing through a gate as the track bends sharply left and starts to go downhill, leave the track to continue in the same direction on a less well trodden path. Walk along the top of the valley, with a wire fence on the right and extensive views on the left, to a gate. Through the gate, follow the fence round to the right and up to an information board. Go ahead a few yards to meet a cross fence.

These downs were acquired by the National Trust from 1977 onwards and more information is given on the board. They have been grazed for over 2,000 years. The Iron Age dyke you will shortly cross is one of several in the area. Their purpose is not clear but they occur where grazing was predominant and may be related to its management.

6. Turn left beside the fence. When the fence ends, cross a depression (in fact an Iron Age dyke) then bear slightly right towards the edge of a wood to find a stile in a fence on the right. Over the stile turn left. Press on in the same direction as a more substantial path joins from the right. Watch for a stile on the left. Do not go over it but at this point bear slightly right downhill, towards Compton Abbas seen nestling below, to reach a gate.

As you look down on Compton Abbas you may be able to pick out the old church tower. The old church was pulled down in 1867 and its tower left. A new church, which you can see ahead and will pass later, was built in 1866 closer to the centre of the village. The old tower apparently had a pear tree growing on top until it blew over in 1945.

7. Through the gate, continue ahead for a little way then bear right across a field to the right-hand one of two gates. Through this gate, follow the path ahead up a slight rise and down the other side. Go through two small metal gates and ahead on a sunken and hedged path to a lane. Note this point as you will return to it after tea.

8. Turn right. Take the first lane on the left. Just before reaching a main road turn left up six steps onto a path parallel with the road. On emerging onto the road, go ahead 50 yards to the teashop on the left.

Compton Abbas is a pretty village of scattered thatched cottages. In 1645 during the Civil War, some Dorset men banded together as the Clubmen. They were opposed to the depredations of both sides in the war. First they attacked the Royalists and then the Parliamentarians and petitioned both sides to stop. Some 2,000 gathered on Hambledon Hill under the command of the rector of Compton Abbas and defied Cromwell. He showed great patience and several times sent emissaries to ask them to lay down their arms. They refused and finally they were routed by 50 of his dragoons. About 300 who didn't run away were imprisoned in Iwerne Courtney church and harangued before they were set free. Cromwell referred to them as 'poor, silly creatures'.

9. Retrace your steps to the point you noted earlier where you joined the lane and now continue ahead along the lane to the main road. This is to avoid walking on the main road as much as possible, though it cannot be eliminated entirely.

10. Turn left for about 1/4 mile.

11. Some 90 yards after a building on the left, turn left over a stile on a path that shortly leads onto a cricket field. Skirt the left-hand side of the field, passing a stile on the left, and at the far end, take a narrow path, following yellow arrows, through a strip of woodland to a stile.

12. Over the stile turn right, along the right-hand side of a field. At the end go left a few yards to a gate whose approach can be extremely muddy. Through the gate turn left. When the fence on the left ends, strike across the field to a stile and continue in the same direction over a second stile onto a lane. Turn right, back to the start.

Walk 9
HOD HILL AND SHILLINGSTONE

*A*s one of the longer and more demanding routes in this book, the walk
described here could be the basis for an all-day expedition exploring one of
the loveliest parts of inland Dorset with a picnic stop or lunch at the White
Horse in Stourpaine, and tea at Shillingstone. We start with a short, sharp
climb up Hod Hill, crowned with the ramparts of an Iron Age fort and
rewarding both for its interest and views. The route then drops down to the
pretty village of Stourpaine and crosses the river Stour to its neighbour,
Durweston, before climbing the other side of the Stour valley through
Blandford Forest. One particularly notable feature of this walk is how
much is in woodland, carpeted with bluebells in spring, shady in summer,
glowing with colour in autumn and majestic in winter. Most of the return
follows the well waymarked Wessex Ridgeway, passing through
Shillingstone with its welcome teashop before a more or less level stretch
back to the start.

The Willows on Blandford Road in Shillingstone is an excellent traditional teashop housed in a 17th-century cob building, originally two farm workers' cottages. In addition to the charming interior, complete with inglenook fireplace, there are some tables outside, shaded by apple trees. All the usual teatime goodies are available including cream teas and a farmhouse tea with a boiled egg. There is an excellent range of delicious cakes temptingly displayed on a sideboard. For lunch, a variety of sandwiches are offered as well as filled jacket potatoes and salads. For a more substantial meal, there is a daily hot selection such as Dorset lamb steak and interesting home-made soup such as avocado, lentil and bacon. The Willows is open between 10 am and 6 pm every day except Monday throughout British Summer Time. In the winter it opens at weekends until 5 pm except in January when it is closed completely. Telephone: 01258 861167.

When the teashop is closed, the White Horse in Stourpaine serves food and there are also, less conveniently, pubs in Shillingstone.

DISTANCE: 7½ miles.

MAP: OS Landranger 194 Dorchester, Weymouth and surrounding area or three Explorer maps — 117 Cerne Abbas and Bere Regis; 118 Shaftesbury and Cranborne Chase; and 129 Yeovil and Sherborne.

STARTING POINT: Hod Hill car park (GR 853112).

HOW TO GET THERE: From the A350 Blandford Forum to Shaftesbury road 1½ miles north of Stourpaine, take a minor road signed 'Hanford 1 Child Okeford 2' to a car park for Hod Hill on the left after about ½ mile.

ALTERNATIVE STARTING POINT: If you wish to visit the teashop at the beginning or end of your walk, start in Shillingstone where some street parking is possible. The teashop is at the south-east end of the village. You will then start the walk at point 16.

THE WALK

1. Leave the rear of the car park and take a path to the left, uphill. As you approach a grassy track bear right on a smaller path to a gate into the fort site.

Hod Hill has the largest internal area of any hillfort in Dorset. It was first fortified in the early Iron Age and further strengthened by more ditches and ramparts in the succeeding centuries. Much of the material used for this came from quarries on the inside. Even today, the inner entrenchment rises to 41 feet above the ditch at one point with a slope of one in two. Vespasian's Second Augustan Legion fought their

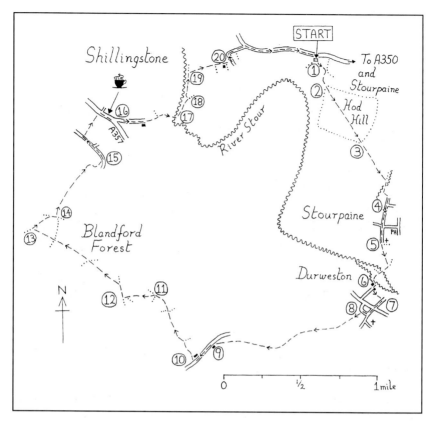

way across Dorset in AD 43, fighting 30 battles. Until they evolved a system for dealing with them, the Romans found the native people quite a handful. The hillforts had formidable defences and the soldiers were very fierce, fighting stark naked and painted bright blue with their hair dressed in spikes with lime. The Romans found the best way was to soften up the inhabitants by bombardment with iron-tipped missiles hurled from a ballista and with fire before attacking under the cover of interlocked shields, called a testudo or tortoise. During excavations many ballista bolts were found near the largest hut, probably that of the chief, suggesting the Romans deliberately targeted it. After their victory, they built a fort inside the ramparts in the corner through which you entered. It was occupied by about 600 foot soldiers and perhaps 250 cavalry — an outpost of empire.

2. Follow the path across the site or, for even better views, round the ramparts to right or left to leave the site at a gate.

Stourpaine.

3. Follow a track downhill to meet a river and turn right beside it, soon crossing to the left bank then turning left into Stourpaine to join a more major road.

4. Continue ahead to the church at the far end of the village where the road finishes. (For the White Horse turn left up to the main road opposite Calf House to the pub on the corner.)

There has been a village here at least since Saxon times and probably longer. After the Norman Conquest, it was taken from Alward, its Saxon owner, and given to a Norman, Humphrey the Chamberlain. It is worth visiting the church to look at the innovative pictorial record of the village's history that has been assembled. It is interesting to compare two views of rural life for which Stourpaine has been used as an example. In 1846 an illustration of the poverty stricken interior of a labourer's cottage was published in the Illustrated London News to show the depths of rural poverty and deprivation. In the 1930s, a romantic view of the village was used to promote St Ivel cheese.

5. Carry on in the same direction on a signed path along the right-hand side of a field and then across a second field to a track. Turn right under a disused railway and ahead over the river Stour, across a meadow then over another branch of the river to a lane by old mill buildings, now restored as dwellings.

6. Turn right. Immediately after a house on the left go over a stile on the left and head along the left-hand side of a field to a second stile and ahead to a lane.

7. Turn right. Cross a main road and continue up the lane opposite. Take the first lane on the right for 70 yards.

Durweston church is dedicated to St Nicholas and was restored in the 19th century. Above the door inside is a 15th-century carving showing one man holding a three legged horse while another shoes a horseless leg. He is probably St Eloy, the patron saint of blacksmiths. Being a saint, he could make life easy for himself by detaching the leg to shoe it. In fact, St Eloy was a goldsmith in France. The king wanted a golden throne and entrusted the work to St Eloy. He found he had been given enough material for two thrones. He gave one to the king, who ordered payment. The saint then produced the second. The monarch was so taken with his honesty that he made St Eloy master of the mint. He was also Bishop of Noyon and died in AD 659.

8. Turn left on a track to two field gates. Go through the one on the left and along the left-hand side of a field and partway along a second to a metal field gate. Through this, continue in the same direction up the valley, now with the field boundary on your right. At the end of the field, the path enters a wood. Carry on through the wood; the path becomes less obvious as the wood thins but press on in the same direction to a field gate out of the wood then ahead to a gate onto a lane by a house.

9. Turn left for about 250 yards.

10. Immediately after a pair of houses on the right, turn right on a track and follow it into a wood, joining a track coming in from the right. The track leads initially along the left-hand side of the wood with a field on the left. When the field ends, ignore a path on the right and then shortly on the left and continue for 250 yards, deeper into the wood to two paths very close together on the left.

11. Turn left on the second of these paths, climbing through the wood, carpeted with bluebells in the spring, to a T-junction with a track.

12. Turn right then branch left after 150 yards. Continue on the track when the wood ends to a cross track in front of another wood.

13. Turn right, passing a path on the left.

14. Take the next path on the left, waymarked as the Wessex Ridgeway and with a blue arrow. Follow this rather rough path steeply down to a lane.

The Ridgeway, one of the great trade routes of Europe, has probably been in use for four thousand years and is one of the oldest roads in the world. It runs from Dorset to the North Sea and rides the back of one of the six great ridges that radiate from Salisbury Plain. It is thought that this ancient route followed the high chalk land to avoid thick forest and marsh and along its length prehistoric remains are found in abundance. The Ridgeway Path is a modern creation. It was proposed by the Ramblers' Association in 1942 and brought into being by the Countryside Commission. In part it runs along the ancient Ridgeway but also uses other paths.

15. Turn left. At a T-junction turn left to carry on in the same direction for 150 yards. Immediately before some newer houses, turn right on a signed bridleway to continue on the Wessex Ridgeway to the A357 in Shillingstone. Turn right to the teashop on the left.

Shillingstone straggles along the A357. Its main claim to fame is that more men per head of population joined up at the outbreak of the First World War than anywhere else in the country. From a total population of 563 men, women and children, 90 men enlisted; 25 did not return. This enthusiastic patriotism was recognised by a congratulatory telegram from King George V.

16. From the teashop turn left for 75 yards then turn left again along Holloway Lane, continuing ahead when this becomes a track after passing a farm. The track ends at a field gate. Through the gate, bear slightly right to a small metal gate and bridge across the river Stour again.

Ahead can be seen two hills, both crowned with hillforts. The one on the right is Hod Hill, climbed at the start of the walk. That on the left is Hambledon Hill. It only has about half the area of Hod Hill but the ramparts are more extensive. This was the site of the Clubmen's stand (see walk 8). The hillsides of forts were kept free of vegetation as a defensive measure with the result that the white chalk was visible. This must have been a particularly impressive view when the forts were in use, especially in sunshine or bright moonlight.

17. Over the bridge, turn left, initially by the river then cutting right across the field to a gate onto a track. Walk along the track for 20 yards.

18. Turn left through a small wooden gate onto a path through a strip of woodland.

19. Watch for a metal gate on the right and turn right through this to walk along the left-hand side of a field. At the end, cross a track and go through the right-hand one of three gates. Walk along a track past farm buildings on the right, over another track and across a field to a lane.

20. Turn left. At a T-junction, turn right, back to the start.

Walk 10
STURMINSTER NEWTON

An ancient and bustling market town, once the home of both Thomas Hardy and the Dorset dialect poet William Barnes, is the focus of this walk in Blackmoor Vale. The route starts with a short climb through Piddles Wood, a fragment of ancient woodland and now a nature reserve. This effort is rewarded by glimpses of attractive views across the Vale to the Downs beyond. We then drop down into the Vale to visit Sturminster's historic mill before tea in the old town square and a gentle stroll back to the start.

The Red Rose Restaurant at Market Cross in Sturminster Newton offers a selection of cakes and delicious desserts as well as cream teas and toasted teacakes. Light lunches, such as sandwiches and things on toast, are available as well as a very reasonably priced three-course meal. Along with the traditional interior, there are a couple of tables outside. Open between

65

9 am and 4.30 pm every day except Sunday throughout the year. Telephone: 01258 472460.

DISTANCE: 4 miles.

MAP: OS Landranger 194 Dorchester, Weymouth and surrounding area or Explorer 129 Yeovil and Sherborne.

STARTING POINT: Fiddleford Manor car park (GR 801135).

HOW TO GET THERE: From the A357 Blandford Forum to Sturminster Newton road a mile east of Sturminster Newton, take a minor road signed 'Fiddleford Manor' to a car park on the left.

ALTERNATIVE STARTING POINT: If you wish to visit the teashop at the beginning or end of your walk, start in Sturminster Newton where there is some street parking and a couple of signed car parks. The teashop is in the centre, overlooking Market Cross. You will then start the walk at point 10.

THE WALK

Note: there is the possibility of mud on the climb through Piddles Wood, so sturdy footwear is advisable.

Fiddlesford Manor, reached by a grassy path from the car park, dates in part from the 14th century and is well worth taking the time to visit if only for its magnificent timber roof. It has been rescued from dereliction by English Heritage and the south end is open to the public (free). Its long and varied history is explained in the building. As well as the roof, note particularly the recently uncovered wall painting in the solar, upstairs, and the intertwined initials of Thomas and Ann White, who did much rebuilding in the 16th century. It is difficult to imagine this rural tranquillity as the scene of riotous drunkenness! The mill by the house was once well known as a hiding place for contraband booze and people apparently flocked from Sturminster for a cheap drink.

1. Turn right out of the car park and walk along the lane to the main road. Turn right for 30 yards then left on a bridleway, signed 'Broad Oak', up through Piddles Wood to a T-junction with a cross path.

Three thousand years ago, almost all of England was covered with temperate rain forest with oak as one of the dominant trees. Down the centuries, this has been cleared until, today, only tiny fragments remain. They were left standing because of their value as a source of timber. Piddles Wood is thought to be one of these fragments. This does not mean that it is untouched, primeval wood, having been managed for timber in the past, but that there has been a wood here for a very long

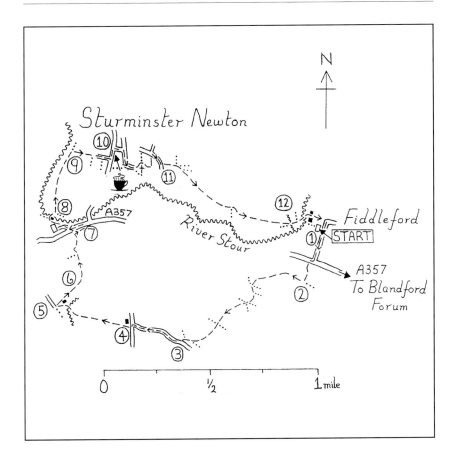

time. As a result, it is particularly valuable for wildlife and is managed as a Nature Reserve by English Nature and Dorset County Council. Information on what may be seen is given on boards.

2. Turn right. Continue ahead on the main track, signed 'Broad Oak ½', at a cross path and ignore all subsequent side paths until you reach a lane.

3. Turn right.

4. At a T-junction bear left across a road to a path to the left of Box Bush House, signed 'Hole House Lane ½'. Keep to the right along this long field to a small gate in the far right corner. This gives onto a

Sturminster Newton mill.

clear path downhill through wood, soon over a footbridge then up to a lane.

5. Turn right in front of the gates of Hole House then turn immediately right again, signed 'Town Bridge ½', to a stile, broken at the time of writing, into a field.

6. The map shows the right of way going diagonally across the field but in practice the path skirts the right perimeter to a stile on the right by a gate. Over the stile, bear half left to a second stile then walk to a third in the far right corner of the field. Go down some steps and continue to a road.

This is Newton, linked to Sturminster by the graceful, arched bridge across the Stour. A notice on it threatens anyone who damages the bridge with transportation for life. Sturminster Castle was near here. It was once the seat of two Saxon kings, Edgar and Edward. The castle was demolished in the 13th century. The Abbots of Glastonbury were lords of the manor from AD 968 until the Dissolution in 1539;

that is the origin of the 'minster' part of the name. They had a building on the site that was given to Catherine Parr, Henry VIII's sixth and last wife. Nothing now remains. The castle is re-incarnated as Stour Castle in Thomas Hardy's novels.

7. Turn left for 140 yards then right along the entrance drive to Sturminster Newton Mill. Bear right at the entrance to the car park to the mill. Take a path to the left of the mill and on across the river.

There has certainly been a mill here since the Middle Ages. The present building dates from the 17th century and was considerably altered in the 19th century. It is open from 11 am until 5 pm between Easter and the end of September on Monday, Thursday, Saturday and Sunday.

8. Go ahead across a field to a gate onto a recreation ground and continue along the left-hand side to meet a surfaced path.

9. Turn right. When the path ends, continue along a road into Sturminster Newton centre to the teashop to the left across a road.

Sturminster Newton has been the market centre of Blackmore Vale at least since the 13th century, a role it serves to this day. On Mondays there is a huge cattle market and the town throngs with farmers doing business. It has a great variety of buildings, reflecting its long history. Many date from the early 18th century after a disastrous fire in 1729. William Barnes, the Dorset dialect poet, was born in 1801 at Rushay Farm, a mile and a half from the town. A local solicitor saw young William drawing a cow on a wheelbarrow he was supposed to be using to clear dung. On enquiring, he found the lad could write a clear hand and was intelligent and so William escaped from the farm into the solicitor's office. He educated himself further, becoming a schoolmaster and then a parson and, towards the end of his life, a friend of the young Thomas Hardy. Barnes wrote poems in Dorset dialect about the countryside he knew and loved. The best known is probably 'Linden Lea', later set to music:

    'An' there vor me the apple tree
    Do lean down low in Linden Lea.'

Thomas Hardy also lived in Sturminster Newton for a couple of years when he was first married — his Sturminster idyll during which he wrote 'The Return of the Native'. His house, Riverside Villa, is just by the recreation ground.

10. From the teashop turn right, right and right again to the church. Pass to the left of the church and at the far end of the churchyard, turn left then turn right at Gotts Corner along a lane for 100 yards.

Fiddleford Manor.

Note minerals, shells and fossils, including three large ammonites, in a wall on the right.

11. Turn left, signed 'Fiddleford Manor and Mill 1'. Follow the path to a stile by a gate. Over the stile, bear right in a field, forking right after 90 yards to another stile by a gate. Now follow the path along the left-hand side of a field then bear right diagonally across the next to a footbridge over a tributary of the river Stour.

12. Cross the corner of a field to a second footbridge over the main river just below a weir. Go ahead between the buildings of Fiddleford Mill and along a drive to a lane. Turn right for a few yards, back to the start.

Walk 11
MILTON ABBAS

This is the longest walk in the book and involves more climbing than most but your efforts will be well rewarded by a series of outstanding views. The route is varied with tracks and lanes, field and woodland paths made especially beautiful in season by sheets of scented bluebells. Tea is at Milton Abbas, an interesting and unusual village, and on the return leg there is the opportunity to visit the abbey church of Milton, still in use as a school chapel.

 The Tea Clipper in Milton Abbas will certainly revive you for the second leg of the walk. It is charmingly housed in one of the village's thatched cottages and has tables outside in a flower-filled courtyard. An excellent range of cakes is served and temptingly displayed and, in addition, cream teas, tasty tarts and other teatime goodies are available. For lunch, quiche, soup and a bake such as lasagne are offered as well as

71

sandwiches, ploughman's and filled jacket potatoes. Everything is home-made. The Tea Clipper opens throughout the summer between 10.30 am and 5.30 pm, closing only on Mondays except Bank Holiday Mondays. In winter it may be open at weekends. Telephone: 01258 880223.

When the teashop is closed, the pub in Milton Abbas, the Hambro Arms, serves food.

DISTANCE: 8 miles.

MAP: OS Landranger 194 Dorchester, Weymouth and surrounding area or Explorer 117 Cerne Abbas and Bere Regis.

STARTING POINT: Bulbarrow Hill viewpoint car park (GR 783059).

HOW TO GET THERE: From the A357 Blandford Forum to Sturminster Newton road 1 mile north of Shillingstone, take a minor road signed 'Okeford Fitzpaine 1'. Through the village, follow the signs to Bulbarrow to two adjacent parking areas on the left.

ALTERNATIVE STARTING POINT: If you wish to visit the teashop at the beginning or end of your walk, start in Milton Abbas where there is some street parking. The teashop is on the main street. You will then start the walk at point 8.

THE WALK

Note: there is one short stretch — see point 5 — where you are in danger of being nettled if a warm summer's day tempts you to walk in shorts.

There are superb, extensive views from Bulbarrow Hill, the second highest point in Dorset at 902 feet. On a clear day you can see over the Vale of Blackmoor as far as Glastonbury and the Quantocks in Somerset. A viewfinder on a pillar helps sort out what is in sight.

1. With your back to the car park turn left along the road then turn left at a road junction. Pass a road on the right to Milton Abbas and continue for 300 yards.

2. Watch for a blue arrow on a post on the right pointing the way to a small gate into a field. This is not at all obvious: if you pass a metal field gate, you have gone 30 yards too far. Head across the field then bear left down into a valley to a wooden gate into a wood. Follow the path through the wood, enjoying the bluebells in season, to leave through another gate and continue along the valley bottom, passing Higher Houghton Farm, after which the path is a surfaced drive.

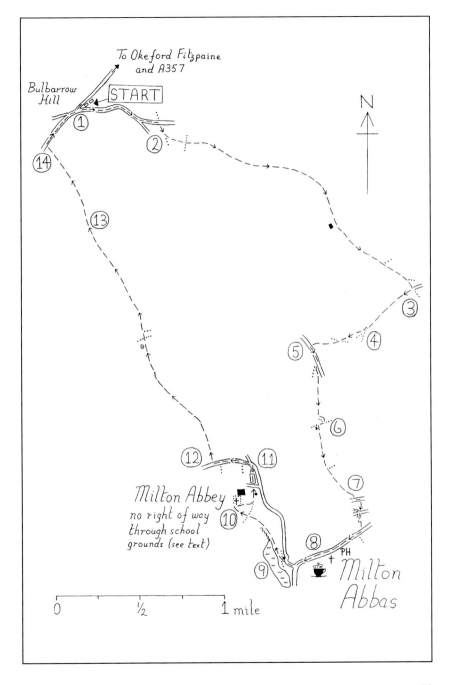

To Okeford Fitzpaine
and A357

Bulbarrow
Hill

START

N

1

2

14

13

3

5

4

6

7

12

11

Milton Abbey
no right of way
through school
grounds (see text)

10

8

PH

9

Milton
Abbas

0   ½   1 mile

Milton Abbey.

3. When the surfaced drive turns sharp left, turn right on a track signed 'Milton Abbas 2½'.

4. Immediately after a gate across the track, go right onto a track from an adjacent field gate. As this track shortly bears left to join the main track, bear right on a clear but much fainter path with outstanding views to the right over the valley you have previously walked down. After about 300 yards a path joins on the left and the path immediately forks. Bear left on the smaller branch to a gate onto a lane.

5. Turn left for 150 yards to a Forest Enterprise track on the right. Do not walk along the track but look at the left-hand side of the track/ road junction for the rather hidden start of a bridleway, marked by a blue arrow on a post. After a short, nettley stretch, the path goes through a small gate into a field. It is not visible on the ground but is waymarked along the right-hand side of a field and then diverted left to a track.

The delightful village of Milton Abbas.

6. Turn right along the track, immediately passing a track on the right. Just before a gatehouse by some imposing gates, turn left on a path, again marked by blue arrows, which leads into and along the right-hand side of a field. Soon extensive views open up ahead and the roofs of Milton Abbas come into view.

7. At the end of the field, go through a small metal gate then bear half left to a small wooden gate and onto a road. Turn left for 50 yards and then right on a grassy path between hedges. At a road turn right then almost immediately left to the end of a cul-de-sac. At the end turn right and follow the path through woods to a road. Turn right, downhill, to the teashop on the left beyond the church.

Milton Abbas is unusual because it was built to a plan. In 1752 the Milton estate came into the hands of Joseph Damer. He had the abbey rebuilt into a magnificent new house but he thought the view was spoiled by the town that had grown up round the abbey. He therefore set about removing it, house by house, as the tenants moved or their leases lapsed and he apparently did not scruple to use excessive encouragement. As can be readily imagined, this action aroused fierce local opposition. One man refused to move and Damer tried to hurry him along by prematurely opening the sluices of the old abbey pond to form a lake. However, he had picked the wrong opponent as the recalcitrant tenant was a lawyer and took Damer to court. He won and all Milton Abbas houses now have a clause in their deeds promising that the lake will not be moved again. When Damer was leaving for London just after the court case, he heard the church bells pealing. It was said they were marking Guy Fawkes Day but he decided it was in celebration of his defeat so he ordered them removed from the tower and sold. Damer's action was arrogant and insensitive but out of it grew an attractive community. He built a new, planned village, out of sight of his house, in the bottom of a steep-sided valley. Some 20 semi-detached, thatched cottages were built; each has an open plan garden in front and a long kitchen garden at the back. There used to be horse-chestnuts between the houses but these were found to be unsafe in 1954 and felled, giving the village its present open appearance. Some of the houses were very overcrowded at one time: there are reports of 36 people living in one, though now both parts often form a single dwelling. In a stroke of good PR, the almshouses were moved from their original site into the new village.

8. From the teashop turn left to continue downhill through the village. At the bottom of the village street, turn right, signed 'Hilton Milton Abbey $\frac{1}{2}$', for about 100 yards to a thatched house on the left.

9. To the left of the thatched house take a gravelled path, signed 'Public footpath to Milton Abbey church only', and follow this to the church.
Note: the public are permitted to walk through the grounds free of charge except during the school Easter and summer holidays, when part of the house is open and an entrance fee is charged. If you are doing this walk during the holidays and do not wish to pay the fee, continue along the road to rejoin the route at point 11.

The abbey was founded in AD 932 by King Athelstan as a college of canons. These were dismissed in AD 964 and replaced by Benedictine monks from Glastonbury. Most of the buildings were destroyed by fire in 1309. A new church was soon begun but not completed before the Dissolution in 1539; the building we see today is only the chancel, tower and transepts. The nave was never built though there are features of the building that show what was planned. There is more information available within. The town of Middleton, later shortened to Milton, grew up round the abbey. It had a grammar school, which was moved to Blandford Forum when Damer razed the town. He claimed that the headmaster had allowed the school building to deteriorate to the point where it was dangerous for pupils. The impecunious headmaster had apparently burned the floorboards and doors as fuel! Damer also complained that the boys stole his fruit and eggs. Thomas Masterman Hardy, later Nelson's Flag Captain, was said to be one of the ringleaders. The building is a school now: no doubt both the buildings and pupils' behaviour are of a higher standard.

After the Dissolution, the estate was bought for the knock-down price of £1,000 by Sir John Tregonwell, a lawyer who had helped Henry VIII divorce Catherine of Aragon. A later John Tregonwell had an astonishing escape. As a child of five, he fell from the church tower. As was the custom in those days, he was wearing stiff Nanking petticoats. These acted as a parachute so he survived unharmed to become High Sheriff of Dorset and die at the age of 82 in 1680. His picture is by the altar in the church. He gave a library of books to the church in thanksgiving for his escape. They disappeared when, it is said, one vicar took them home and his servants used them as hair curling papers.

10. On leaving the church turn left then immediately left again on a gravel path. At the end of the path turn left again and follow the drive through a car park to a road.

The grass staircase of eleven steps, one of only two in England, leads up to a chapel built by the Saxons and rebuilt by the Normans. It is on the site where Athelstan camped on his way to engage the invading Danes. He dreamed he would be victorious, as he was, and he built St Catherine's chapel to commemorate his vision. Next to the staircase is a cottage, one of two left by Damer to provide a touch of rustic charm in his park.

11. Turn left, signed 'Hilton'.

12. Immediately after a wood starts on the right, turn right uphill on a path through the wood that climbs steeply at first and then more gently. Eventually the path leaves the wood. Continue ahead, past a dew pond, and ignore all paths to right and left. This area is a nature reserve. After leaving this at a metal gate, the path is much less distinct. Press on in the same direction, sticking to the left-hand side of two fields and heading towards a communications mast that soon comes into view.

13. After leaving the second field at a metal gate, the path becomes a more distinct track and then a farm drive. Follow this to a lane.

14. Turn right, back to the start.

Walk 12
ATHELHAMPTON

This walk is a chance to compare the works of man and nature. About two thirds of the route uses woodland tracks, which pass some majestic ancient beech trees. As old, or older, than the trees is the focus of this route — the 15th-century manor house of Athelhampton with its superb gardens and excellent teashop. One of the longer walks suggested in this book, it is not particularly arduous: much of the route is on well-made tracks and the ascents are gentle and short. If you enjoy woodland walking, this should be near the top of your list.

 The Coach House Restaurant at Athelhampton is housed at the entrance of an exceptionally attractive building. It successfully combines thatch and glass to give a light and spacious interior and there are some tables outside. For tea there is an excellent range of cakes and pastries including a particularly sticky almond with apricots. Cream teas are served and, if you are feeling very indulgent, why not splash out on the Athelhampton Afternoon Tea, which includes smoked salmon and cucumber sandwiches as well as scones and clotted cream. The lunch menu is tempting and extensive, ranging from snacks such as venison sausage sandwich or croute aux champignons (sautéed mushrooms on a granary crouton) through salads to full meals such as supreme of chicken or lamb cutlets. The Coach House is open every day except Saturday from 10.30 am until 5 pm between March and the end of October and on Sundays in winter. Telephone: 01305 848363.

There is no other source of refreshment on this walk.

DISTANCE: 6¹/₂ miles.

MAP: OS Landranger 194 Dorchester, Weymouth and surrounding area or Explorer 117 Cerne Abbas and Bere Regis or Outdoor Leisure 15 Purbeck and South Dorset.

STARTING POINT: Affpuddle Heath picnic place (GR 804924).

HOW TO GET THERE: From the A35 Dorchester to Bere Regis road about 2 miles west of Bere Regis, take the B3390 towards Warmwell for just under 2 miles to a Forestry Commission car park on the left at a junction with a minor road, signed 'Briantspuddle 1'.

ALTERNATIVE STARTING POINT: If you wish to visit the teashop at the beginning or end of your walk, there is a large car park at Athelhampton but permission should be sought before leaving a car for a long period. The teashop is at the entrance. You will then start the walk at point 9, turning left along the road to a church.

THE WALK

1. Return to the B3390. Take a track opposite for just over ¹/₂ mile, ignoring paths to right and left.

During the last Ice Age, Dorset lay just south of the ice sheet and had a climate similar to the treeless tundra of present day Lapland. As the climate warmed up, starting about 12,000 years ago, trees became established and the area was covered in forest. Eventually, this temperate rain forest was cleared for agriculture. When the light, sandy soil was deprived of its nourishing annual mulch of leaves, it could no longer hold the nutrients and became impoverished, supporting heathland instead of rich farmland. The Bronze Age farmers were the victims of the ecological change they had caused. The heathland stretched right across south-east Dorset and remained an impoverished area for the next 2,000 years. Hardy called it Egdon Heath in his novels and saw it as 'an untameable Ishmaelitish thing, dark and

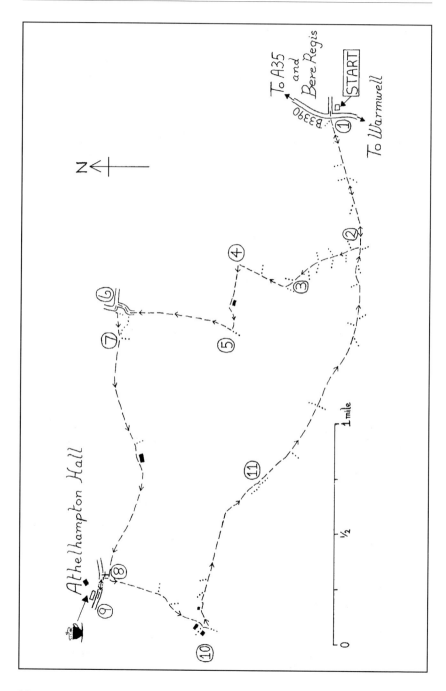

sinister'. Over the last 200 years, Dorset's heaths have been built over, ploughed up, fertilised and reforested, as here, so this area would be unrecognisable to someone from the 18th century. The way of life of a turf cutter of just 200 years ago would be more familiar to someone from the Iron Age than it would to you or me.

2. Turn right on a clear track, waymarked by a blue arrow on a post on the left and passing between two wooden posts. Walk along this track, ignoring all side paths, for about 500 yards. Watch for a major track on the left but **do not turn along it**, instead continue ahead for a further 135 yards.

Even though this wood is a modern creation with many conifers, it is exceptionally attractive and has some magnificent beeches dating from before the modern planting. Beech is a lovely tree with smooth grey bark and glossy green leaves. It is especially beautiful in the spring, when the newly emerged leaves are so fresh, and in autumn when they change from gold to orange to brown. Southern England is the northernmost extent of the beech's range: individual trees are found further north but there are no extensive beech woods. The fruit of the beech is a three-sided nut, sometimes called mast, enclosed in a capsule with quite soft prickles on the outside. Fruit in quantity is produced only in irregular so-called mast years, sometimes at quite long intervals. In other years a late spring frost interferes with the setting of the nuts or a cool summer prevents their ripening. This is one reason why oak is the dominant tree in most of Britain. Notice that many of the beeches are on banks, ancient boundaries that the trees also mark.

3. As the track bears right, look for a blue arrow on a tree and take a smaller path to continue in the same direction, shortly walking just inside the wood. When the main path turns right, continue ahead along the edge of the wood with a wire fence on the left.

4. Turn left through a field gate, waymarked with a blue arrow, and walk with a hedge on the right towards a barn. Pass to the right of the barn, through a field gate then head down to a gate in the far left corner, giving onto a track.

5. Turn right. Continue ahead when the track is surfaced to a T-junction with a lane.

6. Turn left for 30 yards then left again along a signed bridleway. After 20 yards turn right through a small gate to walk along a field to a gate at the far end onto a track.

7. Turn right. Continue along this well-made track past the buildings of Park Farm. When it ends at a turning circle, carry on in the same direction to a stile by a gate and on along the right-hand side of a field. Go through a small gate by a field gate to continue in the same direction, once more on a track.

This is the valley of the Piddle or Puddle, though the river to the right of the track is not at all obvious. Many villages round here take their name from the river, such as Affpuddle and the famous Tolpuddle, where men fought for a decent living for their families in the early 19th century and were severely punished by transportation.

8. At a cross track by a church turn right to a road. Turn left to Athelhampton Hall on the right and the tearoom by the entrance.

The church is relatively modern, dating from 1861. It is now used by the Greek Orthodox community. The delightful, mainly 15th and 16th-century Athelhampton Hall is open to the public at the same times as the teashop. The formal gardens are outstanding with vistas, pools and fountains and a great variety of planting so they are worth seeing at any season. There is also a large circular dovecote. Pigeons used to be kept as a source of meat in the lean days of winter and for their eggs. A suspended ladder allowed the egg collector to move round from hole to hole without having to keep dismounting. Telephone: 01305 848363.

9. Return to the track by the church and turn right along it. Now continue ahead at the junction, climbing gently. At the top follow the path through a wood, passing two obvious paths on the left. Leave the wood through a metal field gate and go towards a farm. Pass to the left of the farm buildings at the bottom of a field to a gate onto a track.

10. Turn left for 30 yards and then sharply left up a track between barbed wire fences towards a thatched cottage. Go through the right-hand one of two gates and head up the left-hand side of a field for 60 yards. Go through a small metal gate on the left and continue in the same direction, just inside a wood, to a gate into a field. Press on in the same direction up the left-hand side of the field to pick up a track leading through a gate into a wood.

11. At the brow of a rise, when the main track bears right, bear left on a smaller track to continue in the same direction and follow this all the way back to the start, rejoining the outward route for the final ¹/₂ mile.

The rhododendrons are an attractive sight when they are in bloom but conservationists regard them as a pernicious weed and spend much time 'rhodie bashing'. The reason is that they are not native species, having been imported as garden plants from India. The mild, damp British climate suits them very well and they have escaped from gardens to colonise woods. Being an alien species, they do not support the wide range of insects and birds that depend on the native species such as holly and hazel, which they have supplanted. In addition, their thick, evergreen leaves shade out the woodland flowers that otherwise would grow on the forest floor.

Walk 13
CERNE ABBAS

Starting close to the best viewpoint of the famous, and somewhat startling, naked Giant of Cerne Abbas, this short but energetic walk explores the hills overlooking the town. There is some magnificent downland walking with outstanding views. The route then passes beneath the feet of the Giant before visiting the ancient community of Cerne Abbas where you can refresh yourself with water from a well which reputedly has magical properties as well as with tea. A short stroll brings you back to the start.

The Singing Kettle on Long Street in Cerne Abbas is a charming traditional teashop housed in a Grade II listed building dating from 1750. At the rear is a pleasant garden where you can enjoy your tea in clement weather. A tempting range of cakes is offered including a delicious Dorset apple cake served warm with clotted cream and, of course, cream teas are available. Possibilities for lunch range from light snacks such as sandwiches or soup to full meals such as ham and eggs or broccoli and cheese bake. The Singing Kettle is open every day except Monday between 10.30 am and 5.30 pm. Telephone: 01300 341349.

DISTANCE: 4 miles.

MAP: OS Landranger 194 Dorchester, Weymouth and surrounding area or Explorer 117 Cerne Abbas and Bere Regis.

STARTING POINT: Kettle Bridge picnic area near Cerne Abbas (GR 883015).

HOW TO GET THERE: From the A352 Dorchester to Sherborne road 11 miles south of Sherborne and 8 miles north of Dorchester, by a small parking area for the Giant viewpoint, take a minor road signed 'Cerne Abbas' then the first on the left, following the signs to Kettle Bridge picnic area.

ALTERNATIVE STARTING POINT: If you wish to visit the teashop at the beginning or end of your walk, start in Cerne Abbas where it may be possible to park on the main street where the teashop is to be found. You will then start the walk at point 10.

THE WALK

Note: Be warned: this is not a walk for shorts in the summer months as there are some nettley stretches.

1. Turn right out of the car park, right at a T-junction and right again at the main road.

The layby on the main road is the best spot from which to view the celebrated Giant — far enough away to see the whole figure but near enough to see the detail. Some, perhaps most, authorities claim he dates from Roman times and is a representation of Hercules. Others say he is the Celtic god Nodons and so even earlier. Yet others assert he is much more recent, dating from perhaps the 18th century. Certainly, as essentially nothing more than a scratching in the chalk, he would need regular cleaning up to stay visible but there is no mention of him until the 18th century. The first record in print was in the Gentleman's Magazine of 1764. Many later depictions omit his most obvious feature (and I don't mean his club!), presumably on grounds of modesty. Writers felt they had to make some mention. One referred to 'indications of phallic corruption to which worship of the all-vivifying sun invariably led': an invitation to sun worship if ever there was one! Spending the night on the Giant has been recognised as a cure for infertility, a practice the National Trust try to discourage. Unfortunately, he has been fenced in for his own protection which makes him look as if he is being offered up on a tray in aerial photographs.

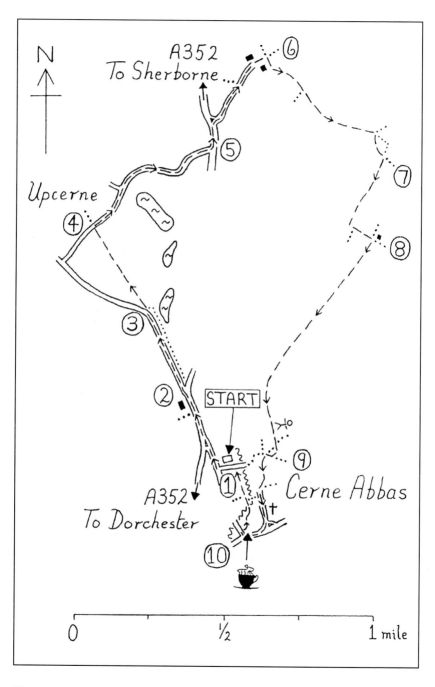

The Cerne Abbas Giant.

2. When the road bears right after 300 yards, bear left along a lane signed 'Upcerne' and follow it as far as some white gates on the right.

The large, somewhat grim building on the left just before the junction was the workhouse, one of a dozen built in Dorset in the 1830s as part of the Government's answer to extensive rural poverty following the Napoleonic Wars. Today, it is a nursing home.

3. Climb over a stile to the left of the gates and follow the signed path ahead across a field to rejoin the lane.

4. Turn right. At the hamlet of Upcerne continue ahead, ignoring a lane on the left.

Upcerne enjoys a wonderful situation in a bowl of chalk downland. Arthur Mee, writing in 1939, eulogised: 'it lies among the downs smiling to itself like a child in hiding delighted that the highroad (sic) passes so near yet misses it'. He added 'the great world passes it by', as it still does.

5. At the main road turn left for 150 yards then turn right, signed 'Minterne Parva only'. Continue past farm buildings to a cross track.

6. Turn right, signed 'Bridleway to Giants Head'. When the main track bends right, continue ahead on a less well used track, marked by a blue arrow on a post. The track soon ends; carry on across a field to a small metal gate. Through the gate, follow the by now quite faint path round to the right, bearing right at two forks to come to another small gate. It is worth pausing as you climb to admire the stunning views that are gradually revealed.

7. Do not go through the second small gate but turn right on an unsigned path along the top of a very steep slope. This eventually swings left to climb again to a barn at the top of the hill.

8. Turn right on a signed path. This path starts by crossing a field but there soon follows a lovely stretch of downland walking, gradually dropping down the hillside. The path leads beneath the feet of the Giant then shortly to a cross path.

Along this path, between the top of the down and the Giant's head, you pass the site of an ancient enclosure called the Trendle or the Giant's Frying Pan. A maypole was erected here on May Day and it was the scene of much merry making, with the resulting pregnancies no doubt blamed on the Giant, until the Puritans put a stop to it all in 1635.

9. Go over a stile at a fence corner into a field ahead and bear half right to an arched gate. Follow the path across the graveyard to a lane. Turn left into Cerne Abbas, turning right at a T-junction to the teashop on the right.

The abbey, from which Cerne Abbas gets its name, was established in AD 987 and the town grew up around it. Almost nothing remains today. The abbey church was probably on the site of the graveyard and the humps in the field you walked across may be remains of some of the buildings. Only two structures remain, the porch to the Abbots Hall and the guest house. They are open to the public in summer (telephone: 01300 341284). The church on the left was built by the monks for the town in the 14th century and has more information available within.

At the end of the graveyard a path to the left leads to St Augustine's Well, once the town's water supply. It is surrounded by legends. For example, one says that St Augustine asked local shepherds whether they would prefer their thirst to be quenched by beer or water. When they virtuously chose water, he struck the ground with his staff and water gushed forth. It is supposed to have healing properties and still flows today, feeding the picture postcard duck pond.

The church and duck pond are on Abbey Street. The buildings are thought to have been constructed in the 15th century, possibly as abbey buildings, though they have obviously undergone many alterations down the centuries. At the end is the Pitchmarket where farmers would display samples of corn for inspection by purchasers. Abbey Street was the home of one Thomas Washington, said to be the uncle of George Washington. Certainly there is a connection between the town and the government of the United States. A family called Notley emigrated in the 17th century and held land they called Cerne Manor. In the 18th century this became Capitol Hill, seat of the new federal government.

10. After tea turn right along Duck Street for 20 yards then right along Mill Lane (or leave the teashop through the garden gate and turn right). Immediately after Mill House, bear right to walk with a stream on your left. The path soon crosses the stream. Continue beside it to a second bridge. Do not cross this but turn left, back to the start.

The community has seen many changes down the centuries. After the abbey was dissolved, Cerne Abbas was a market town with thriving leather and brewing trades. The Hodges, for example, from their premises in Abbey Street, were shoemakers to Walter Raleigh, George III and the young Queen Victoria. However, the railway passed the town by and hastened a decline; the last mail coach stopped at the New Inn in 1855. The population fell by a half in 50 years and, writing in the early years of the 20th century, one author said, 'If you would make the acquaintance of a dead town, allow me to introduce you to Cerne Abbas. It is a weary, age-worn place, a little off the main road, and rapidly falling into decay.' Now, of course, the cycle has turned again and Cerne is once more prosperous with the tourist trade and as a dormitory community.

Walk 14
PORTLAND

Portland is Dorset's own Gibraltar — a rocky eminence with a strong military presence. It is quite unlike the rest of the county with a totally different atmosphere and is heavily scarred by quarrying to win the valuable Portland stone. This walk starts by crossing the 'Island' on a path between two working quarries, not beautiful but very interesting. The rest of the route is an exhilarating cliff walk with extensive views of the Dorset coast and even as far as Devon. It passes Portland Bill, well known from the shipping forecasts, where the famous lighthouse is open to visitors.

The Lobster Pot at Portland Bill is more of a restaurant than a traditional teashop. It offers a wide range of full meals, including crab and other salads as well as things with chips. Excellent cream teas are served alongside cakes, ice creams and a very tasty gooseberry tart. The pleasant modern building has views over the sea to one side and tables outside. It is open all

day, every day from March to November. Telephone: 01305 820242.
When the teashop is closed, the pub at Portland Bill, the Pulpit,
serves food.

DISTANCE: 4½ miles.
MAP: OS Landranger 194 Dorchester, Weymouth and surrounding area or Outdoor
Leisure 15 Purbeck and South Dorset.
STARTING POINT: Cheyne Weares car park (GR 693705).
HOW TO GET THERE: From the A354 from Weymouth across the bridge to
Portland and continue through Fortuneswell and Easton, following the signs to
Portland Bill, to Cheyne Weares car park on the left.
ALTERNATIVE STARTING POINT: If you wish to visit the teashop at the beginning
or end of your walk, start at Portland Bill where there is ample parking (charge).
The teashop is by the car park. You will then start the walk at point 6.

THE WALK
1. Return to the road and turn left for 300 yards.

2. Turn right on a signed path, going through a gate to the left of the
main quarry gates and straight ahead to pick up a path between two
quarry roads, walking with a wire fence on your right. Cross two
quarry tracks and continue on the path to eventually emerge by an
electricity sub-station on a road.

*Portland is a bit of England spread all over England — and beyond. The fine
qualities of Portland stone, white, resistant but soft enough to carve, were first
recognised by Inigo Jones when he built the Banqueting Hall in Whitehall in the
early 17th century. Enormous quantities have been used since then in many of
England's finest buildings including St Paul's, the Bank of England, the British
Museum and the Cenotaph. Quarrying has left scars all over the island so it can
hardly be called beautiful, but it is interesting to see how nature triumphs in even
these adverse circumstances. Opportunistic plants thrive in the disturbed ground by
the path through the quarry and in summer it is a mass of flowers.*

3. Turn left.

4. At a T-junction go straight ahead on a path signed 'Barleycrates
Lane' and walk along the clear main path to the cliffs, ignoring a path
on the right at a left-hand bend.

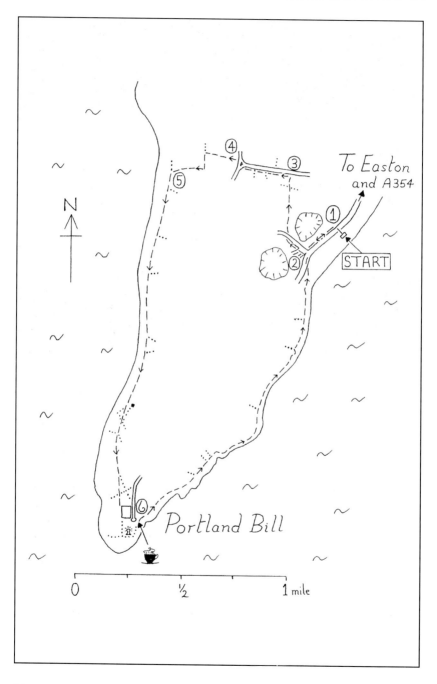

To Easton
and A354

START

N

Portland Bill

0   ½   1 mile

The lighthouse at Portland Bill.

Portland illustrates how limestone resists erosion by the sea. It is not truly an island, being connected to the mainland by Chesil Beach and by a bridge, which replaced the ferry in 1839. Its isolation produced a rugged independence among its native people. Writing in 1906, Frederick Treves said, '...they married only with their own folk, and possessed curious laws and still more curious morals'. Along with quarrying and agriculture, wrecking was a traditional occupation and every great storm brought a vessel to plunder. It is not surprising that smuggling was also rife; between 1817 and 1845, 129 islanders are listed in the registers of Dorchester prison for smuggling related offences, more than any other Dorset community. The islanders were well known for their ability with the sling and Customs men were reluctant to carry out their duty at Portland, 'for fear of being knocked on the head by a volley of stones', said an 18th-century report.

5. Turn left and follow the broad, grassy path to the tip of Portland to find the teashop to the left of the car park for Portland Bill.

Portland Bill is the low nose at the end of the island that projects into the English

93

Channel. Of the three lighthouses, the old one you pass is a private house, once owned by Marie Stopes (of birth control fame). The other disused lighthouse is a bird observatory where censuses of migrating birds are made. The one in use is open to the public every day except Saturday between 11 am and 5 pm (charge). The climb of 153 steps is worth making, if you have the energy, to see the massive light and the extensive views. The disturbed area of sea off Portland Bill is The Race, very dangerous for shipping.

6. After exploring Portland Bill, take the path to the seaward side of the Lobster Pot and follow it along the cliffs, soon passing through a colony of huts. Carry on along this path, eventually passing the cliff top and walking through a disused quarry. Ignore all paths to the left until the main path eventually leads back up to the road. Turn right, back to the start.

There are several interesting things to see from the path. The colony of huts belong to local people and are now used as sort of beach huts. Some of them were recently moved to improve the view of the sea from the car park. Behind them can be seen the remains of medieval strip cultivation. On the sea side, notice the ledge partway down the cliff. This is a raised beach, representing the sea level 120,000 years ago. There is also a cave where the roof has fallen in, making a blow hole, now covered by slabs for safety reasons. All the early quarries were on the coast and the stone was manoeuvred directly into boats. The derricks along the cliff edge today are to raise and lower boats.

Walk 15
ABBOTSBURY

This route comes very close to the ideal teashop walk. It leads through attractive countryside with plenty of interesting natural history to observe on the way. A short climb gives splendid views of the West Dorset coastline in both directions and also inland. Then, just when we are beginning to flag, an ancient village is encountered, an excellent place to stop for tea. Fully refreshed, we can enjoy the historic buildings before an easy, downhill stroll leads back to the start.

Wheelwrights is a charming traditional teashop whose name reflects the history of the building. It was a wheelwright's for 400 years and you may notice that the floors slope towards the road to allow access for carts and wagons. It then became a potter's and glass engraver's, resulting in the large, interesting window facing the street. After a spell as a baker's, the building became the teashop we see today. A variety of cakes are available as well as cream teas. A range of teas is offered with a changing selection of fruit teas. For a light lunch, served between noon and 2 pm, ploughman's, quiche or cheese rolls with salad are available. The interior is decorated with a display of textiles, some of which are the owner's own, as well as a changing display of other artists' work. There are some tables, made from treadle sewing machines, in the pleasant garden. Wheelwrights is open every day from Wednesday to Sunday and Bank Holiday Mondays throughout the year between 10.30 am and 5 pm. Telephone: 01305 871800.

When this teashop is closed, there are several other teashops and pubs in Abbotsbury.

DISTANCE: 4½ miles.

MAP: OS Landranger 194 Dorchester, Weymouth and surrounding area or Outdoor Leisure 15 Purbeck and South Dorset.

STARTING POINT: Abbotsbury beach car park, for which there is a charge (GR 560846).

HOW TO GET THERE: From the B3157 Weymouth/Bridport road ½ mile west of Abbotsbury, take a minor road signed 'Sub-tropical Gardens ¼ Chesil Beach ¾' to the beach car park on the left.

ALTERNATIVE STARTING POINT: If you wish to visit the teashop at the beginning or end of your walk, start in Abbotsbury where there is ample parking in the village car park (charge). The teashop is to the left from the car park. You will then start the walk at point 8.

THE WALK

1. Leave the car park by a board walk to the left of the public lavatories and beach café and turn left on a path behind the pebble bank. It is heavy going, scrunching through the pebbles, but it soon becomes easier as a path develops. Keep left as the path diverges from the beach and is enclosed between a tamarisk hedge and fence.

Chesil Beach (see walk 16) is separated from the land by a brackish lagoon called The Fleet for most of its length. The Fleet is 7¾ miles long and opens to the sea at Portland. Its mud banks harbour rich marine life and it is an excellent sanctuary for birds on this wild coast.

2. Watch for a stile on the right next to a metal field gate. Climb this and walk along the right-hand side of two fields on a permissive path. Towards the end of the second field, bear left to a stile 25 yards to the left of a gate. Over the stile, continue ahead along the right-hand side of a third field, following the boundary round to a stile.

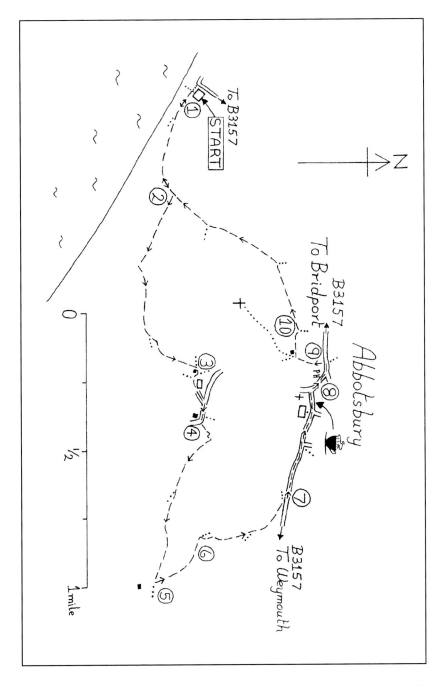

Over the stile, walk past the Swannery restaurant (too early for tea!) to a track.

3. Turn right, passing the entrance to the Swannery on the right and a car park on the left, to reach a road. Turn right for 200 yards.

The population of swans has been managed since there was a monastery at Abbotsbury when it provided the monks with a source of meat. The swans thrive on a rare eel grass that grows here. The birds are wild and are encouraged to come by the provision of food and nesting materials. The Swannery is open to the public every day between Easter and the end of October from 10 am until 6 pm (telephone: 01305 871858).

4. As the road bends right, immediately after farm buildings on the right, turn left, going to the right of some double farm gates, to pick up a path along the left-hand side of a field. At the top of the field, cross a stile then bear round to the right and climb a hill, guided by occasional posts. At the top, go over a stile and continue as the path levels out with a fence on the left.

There are splendid wide-ranging views from this vantage point. Across Lyme Bay to the west they stretch as far as Devon. The view of Chesil Beach with The Fleet behind and the Isle of Portland beyond is particularly good while inland the hills and valleys, woods and streams of the Dorset countryside are a delight.

5. Level with a farm below, turn left on a signed path along the right-hand side of a field that goes uphill and down dale to a gate on the right-hand side into woodland.

6. Through the gate, go ahead to pass to the left of a metal structure then follow the path to the left and downhill through the wood to a gate into a field. Continue ahead, still downhill, to the left-hand one of two gates onto a track and walk along this to a road.

 7. Turn left into Abbotsbury and the teashop on the right.

Abbotsbury is exceptionally attractive and pains are taken to keep it so. Notice on the right as you walk into the village that new buildings are designed to blend with the old. Many of the buildings date from the 17th and 18th centuries and are built of local stone. If you look closely, you will be able to pick out carved and dressed stones robbed from the abbey.

Abbotsbury.

8. Turn right out of the teashop to continue along the road through the village, staying on the main road (West Street) and passing Strangways Hall and the Ilchester Arms.

Abbotsbury was already in the possession of the Abbot of Glastonbury when the land was given by King Canute to his steward, Orc, who endowed the monastery with great wealth. The monks lived well, as can be seen from the enormous tithe barn, built to hold the taxes of a tenth of produce. The barn is the largest in England and still stands. Today, it holds the unlikely but interesting exhibit of reproductions of the terracotta warriors from China! The village grew and prospered with the monastery but the end came in 1539 with the Dissolution. The estate passed to the Strangways family, who have held it ever since. Much of the fabric of the abbey went to build the Strangways' mansion and some into local cottages. In the Civil War, the Strangways were for the King. Their house was besieged and taken by Parliamentary troops. The commander ordered the house to be fired but his own troops, reckless or ignorant of the gunpowder stored within, were plundering it and were blown up with the house when the gunpowder exploded. Nothing remains today except a bit of wall. There is also evidence of the fighting in the church, which has two bullet holes in the pulpit.

9. Turn left at a cross track, Chapel Lane, and continue along the track to a T-junction. Follow the main path round to the right at a barn, where a path ahead leads up to the chapel high on the hill.

St Catherine's chapel stands on a steep, 250 foot hill but it is well worth the 10 minute climb for the views from the top. It was built by the abbey in the 15th century and its walls are 4 feet thick. St Catherine is the patron saint of spinsters and they would come here to pray:

> *'A husband, St Catherine;*
> *A handsome one, St Catherine;*
> *A rich one, St Catherine;*
> *A nice one, St Catherine;*
> *And soon, St Catherine!'*

The chapel survived the Dissolution because of its value as a landmark and lookout.

10. At a T-junction turn left. Turn left again at the next T-junction and follow the path back to the start, rejoining the outward route for the last few hundred yards.

Walk 16
WEST BAY AND BURTON BRADSTOCK

This walk sets off eastwards with a gentle stroll before tea and then continues with a more strenuous return route along a switch-back cliff path. Walking this way round, you are heading westwards on the coast path between Burton Beach and West Bay and will be able to make the most of some outstanding views of the West Dorset coastline. The views backwards, of Chesil Beach with The Fleet behind, are also good and you will find plenty of opportunities to turn and enjoy them while climbing the cliffs.

Hive Beach Café at Burton Bradstock is a particularly superior beach café housed in a very attractive modern building with plenty of tables outside overlooking the sea. A good array of tasty cakes is temptingly displayed and, of course, cream teas are available. For full meals the accent is definitely on fish, including a speciality fish soup and crab salad. For a lighter meal there are sandwiches, including delicious bacon butties, and filled jacket potatoes. It is open every day between 10 am and 5 pm except during December and January. As well as the café, there is a separate ice cream parlour with an interesting range of ices such as sticky toffee fudge, hive honeycomb and Beaulieu blackberry. Telephone: 01308 897070.

When the teashop is closed, pubs in Burton Bradstock and West Bay serve food.

DISTANCE: 4 miles.
MAP: OS Landranger 193 Taunton and Lyme Regis or Outdoor Leisure 15 Purbeck and South Dorset.
STARTING POINT: Station Yard car park, West Bay (GR 465904).
HOW TO GET THERE: From the Crown Inn roundabout on the A35 just south of Bridport, take the B3157, signed 'West Bay'. On a right-hand bend, just before the harbour, turn left to a car park on the left just beyond the West Bay Hotel.
ALTERNATIVE STARTING POINT: If you wish to visit the teashop at the beginning or end of your walk, start at Burton Bradstock beach car park. The teashop overlooks the sea. You will then start the walk at point 9.

THE WALK

Before starting the walk, it is worth turning right to have a look at the harbour. West Bay is the port of Bridport and there has been a harbour here for a long time; Joan of Navarre landed here on her way to marry Henry IV. It is entirely artificial, being built in the estuary of the river Brit, and has been substantially reconstructed and repaired down the centuries. The river is held back by sluices under the road bridge to scour the harbour at low tide. West Bay used to be called Bridport Harbour. When the railway came in 1884, it had aspirations to become a seaside resort and perhaps its original name did not attract the tourists.

1. Return to the road and turn left for about 200 yards, as far as the entrance to a golf club.

2. Turn right along the entrance drive and follow this up round a sharp left-hand bend and as far as a sharp right-hand bend.

3. At this point leave the drive and take a narrow, unsigned path on the left that climbs to meet a fence on the left. Follow the fence to the left and walk beside it as far as the top of a pronounced dip.

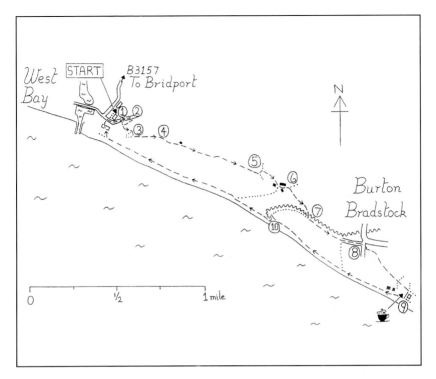

The definitive path, as shown on the Ordnance Survey map, is impassable. The first part of the route across the golf course is open by the agreement of the golf club.

4. Bear right away from the fence and along the top of a steep slope to pass to the right of huts seen ahead to pick up a track. Follow this across the golf course to a caravan site. Note the ammonite on top of a wall on the left.

5. Turn left through a gate into a caravan site then right down through the site. Follow the drive between buildings and left round onto a camping field.

6. When the wall on the right ends, turn right across the field to a fingerpost on the far side to pick up a path signed 'Burton Bradstock ¹/₂ Abbotsbury 8'. Cross a field to a footbridge across a river.

In the ninth century a Burton Bradstock fisherman, watching for mackerel, saw the Danes coming. This gave the men of the village time to prepare an ambush and the

Danes were massacred. It is said the river ran red with Danish blood and this was known as Red Bottom.

7. Over the bridge, turn left. When the path ends, continue ahead along a lane to a T-junction.

Most of Burton Bradstock lies to the left, over the river. It is one of many villages that save their best for those who explore on foot, with a network of lanes lined by pretty thatched cottages, many dating from the 17th and 18th centuries and built of local stone. It was originally called Bridetun — the farm on the river Bride. The addition of Bradstock comes from the Wiltshire abbey of Bradenstoke, which owned the manor in the 13th century.

8. Turn right for 10 yards then go left on an unsigned path up some stone steps. At the top cross a stile and follow a path initially along the left-hand side of a field then right across it to a wooden kissing gate next to a field gate, heading just to the left of two buildings. Continue in the same direction across a second field to another kissing gate and on over a third to the entrance to a car park. Turn right along a track to the teashop.

9. From the teashop turn right along the coast path.

At Burton Beach the geology of the cliffs changes. To the west the cliffs are sandstone, which forms higher cliffs than the softer clay rocks to the east.

10. When the path reaches the beach, do not turn right as indicated by the sign. Instead, turn left below the cliffs to cross the river at a pebble bar. Now turn right to scrunch your way across the beach. At the end of the caravan site climb up the cliff path to continue over the next cliff to West Bay. Turn right, back to the car park.

(Note: if the beach route is impassable for any reason, turn right as signed, which will lead you back to the bridge over the river crossed earlier in the walk. Over the bridge, turn left and follow the right of way through the caravan site to rejoin the cliff path.)

Chesil Beach is unique in Europe. It is an ever-changing bank of pebbles, which extends 18 miles east from Burton Bradstock to Portland. One of the most remarkable things about it is that the pebbles are graded with small ones at this end to much larger ones at the other: it is said that smugglers and others could tell just

West Bay harbour.

where they were by looking at the pebbles. It is a dangerous place. Swimming is always treacherous and it has a long history of wrecks. In 1824 an ordnance sloop was carried bodily onto the ridge and the crew just disembarked and walked into Portland! Many others have not been so fortunate. All manner of objects have been cast ashore, from ships' boilers to silver ingots, including, in 1757, a mermaid. She was no beauty, according to those who saw her. There are many theories about the origin of this unique geological feature but none are entirely satisfactory. The pebbles have come partly from flint beds in the chalk on the floor of the English Channel and partly from the cliffs of West Dorset. One suggestion is that, as the sea level rose at the end of the last Ice Age, the bank of pebbles was rolled forward until it was halted by the land. What is not explained is why it should form just here, along this relatively short stretch of coast, nor why the pebbles are sorted by size.

Walk 17
BRADPOLE AND MANGERTON MILL

Nestling in a fold of the West Dorset hills, Mangerton is a tiny hamlet in the tranquil valley of the river Manger. This charming short walk starts at Bradpole on the outskirts of Bridport and first visits the attractive village of Loders before ancient tracks and paths through fields and woods lead over the hill to Mangerton. The return is an easy walk on a quiet field path beside the river. A pleasant stroll for a summer's afternoon — or any season.

The peaceful valley of the Manger is the setting for this delightful traditional tearoom housed in a restored 17th-century working water mill. As well as the charming interior, there are tables outside so you can enjoy your food overlooking the mill pond, with the sound of the water wheel turning. A welcome, and unusual, feature is to offer cream teas of three different sizes to cater for different appetites. The Mangerton tea is more savoury with a cheese scone and slice of tea bread. Other set teas include a country tea with cucumber sandwiches and cake and a children's tea with Marmite or peanut butter. In addition, there is a good selection of tempting cakes, including Dorset apple cake. Lunch is served between noon and 2 pm and includes sandwiches, filled jacket potatoes, salads and omelettes as well as a more substantial daily special. Mangerton Mill Tea Room is open every day on Tuesday to Sunday and Bank Holiday Mondays from Good Friday until October between 11 am and 5.30 pm. In October, it is open afternoons only between 2 pm and 5 pm. Telephone: 01308 485224.

When the teashop is closed, the Loders Arms, in Loders, serves excellent food.

DISTANCE: 3¹/₂ miles.
MAP: OS Landranger 193 Taunton and Lyme Regis or Explorer 117 Cerne Abbas and Bere Regis.
STARTING POINT: Car park in Bradpole (GR 482941).
HOW TO GET THERE: From the A3066 Bridport to Beaminster road at the Kings Head just on the outskirts of Bridport, take a minor road signed 'Bradpole'. Fork right at the church to a small car park on the right, just before the post office on the left.
ALTERNATIVE STARTING POINT: If you wish to visit the teashop at the beginning or end of your walk, start at Mangerton Mill, either parking in the car park after seeking permission, or you might be able to find a roadside spot. You will then start the walk at point 12.

THE WALK

The ancient community of Bradpole is now almost a suburb of Bridport. Its most distinguished son is W. E. Forster. He introduced the Education Bill into Parliament in 1870, which established free, universal education.

1. Turn right out of the car park, then left at a T-junction.

2. Turn right at the next T-junction for ¹/₄ mile.

3. Turn right on a surfaced drive and walk along it to a farm, passing between farm buildings.

4. Immediately after the farmhouse on the left, turn left on a broad, grassy path. When this peters out in a field, bear half left to a metal kissing gate then follow the path up to a road.

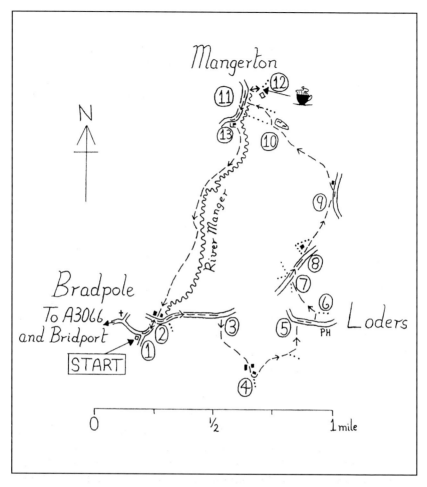

This is Loders, an attractive village that grew around a priory of which only the church remains. It is said that in Tudor times a miserly resident buried his money so no one else should enjoy it. Some 400 years later, a boy was taking up the floor of a barn and discovered a pot containing hundreds of silver pieces.

5. Turn right for 100 yards then turn left along a bridleway on a surfaced track to the left of Hinkhams, opposite The Farmers Arms (no longer a pub). When the track soon ends, head up a hedged path to a T-junction with a cross path.

6. Turn left up a deep, sunken path to a lane.

7. Turn right for about 250 yards.

8. Turn left along the surfaced drive for Cloverleaf Farm. The right of way is immediately to the right. The Dorset County Council arrow is badly angled and many people go to the left of the house into the farmyard then right. Either way, make your way across a field to a gap in a hedge. In the next field, bear half left, passing to the right of a pylon, to a gate onto a lane.

9. Turn left for 40 yards then left on a bridleway to the left of a building and follow the path just inside a wood.

10. Just after a very large pond in a field on the right and immediately before a gate out of the wood, fork right downhill to a stile then bear half left until you meet a track. Turn left along it to a gate onto a lane.

 11. Turn right for 70 yards then right again to the teashop.

The mill is thought to have been built in the late 17th century and was working until the late 1960s, grinding barley and oats for animal feed. It then fell into disrepair until the present owners bought it in 1986. They are steadily restoring it and have brought the water wheel back into operation.

12. Return to the road and turn left.

13. Immediately after a house called 'Sunnymead', turn left through a metal gate and then left again. Turn right to a stile in the far right corner. Now follow the path across fields with the river on the left. The path is not visible on the ground at the time of writing but is easy to navigate from stile to stile and is well waymarked. At one point, it crosses the fence on the left to pass through a short stretch of wood before resuming its course across fields to eventually pass between farm buildings and emerge on a lane. Take the lane almost opposite, back to the start.

Walk 18
MAPPERTON AND BEAMINSTER

West Dorset is exceptionally attractive, with steep-sided valleys dissecting rolling hills, and deserves to be better known by walkers. This route explores the hills and vales to the east of Beaminster, calling in at the ancient town for refreshment. There is plenty of historic interest: we pass two stately homes and a village devastated by the Great Plague with a poignant reminder of those sad times.

Ann Day is a local artist specialising in bold, confident watercolours and these are displayed in a gallery in Beaminster that incorporates a most attractive modern café since Ann has the sense to be married to a master baker. My recommendation is to organise the day to have lunch at the Ann Day Gallery. Excellent soup with crusty bread, Dorset rarebit and interesting salads are on offer. The range of cakes includes a delicious Dorset apple cake as well as a wicked treacle tart, making this establishment popular with visitors and residents alike. In summer it is open every day until 5 pm except Saturday when it closes at 2.30 pm and Sunday when it is closed. Between October and May it closes every day at 2.30 pm. Telephone 01308 863658.

When the teashop is closed, there are several other cafés and pubs in Beaminster.

DISTANCE: 4¹/₂ miles.
MAP: OS Landranger 193 Taunton and Lyme Regis and 194 Dorchester, Weymouth and surrounding area or Explorer 117 Cerne Abbas and Bere Regis.
STARTING POINT: Layby on the A3066 immediately north of the entrance to Parnham House, ¹/₂ mile south of Beaminster (GR 478003).
HOW TO GET THERE: Take the A3066 Bridport to Beaminster road to a layby about ¹/₂ mile south of Beaminster on the west side of the road.
ALTERNATIVE STARTING POINT: If you wish to visit the teashop at the beginning or end of your walk, start in Beaminster, parking in the car park in Fleet Street or in the square. The tea shop is on Hogshill Street, off the square. You will then start the walk at point 10.

THE WALK

1. Facing the road, turn right for 150 yards, passing the entrance to Parnham House. Turn left on a signed bridleway along a drive and follow it through a farmyard.

2. After the last farm building, a track leads up to a house ahead. Do not take this but take a signed path to the left of, and parallel with, the track.

3. At the top, turn right on a cross path, following the signs for the Jubilee Trail. The path soon joins a parallel track. Follow this for about a mile to a junction with a lane.

Mapperton was ravaged by the bubonic plague. In September 1666 the survivors met by the tree at the junction of the track and the lane. It is called The Posy Tree because they carried posies of flowers and herbs, which were widely believed to ward off the disease. They are referred to in the nursery rhyme:
'Ring-a-ring of roses' (the rosy rash typical of the disease)
'Pocket full of posies' (posies to ward off the disease)
'Atishoo, Atishoo' (sneezing when the disease reaches the lungs)
'We all fall down' (very high mortality rate among plague victims).
The present tree is, of course, a descendant of the original. People from Mapperton

111

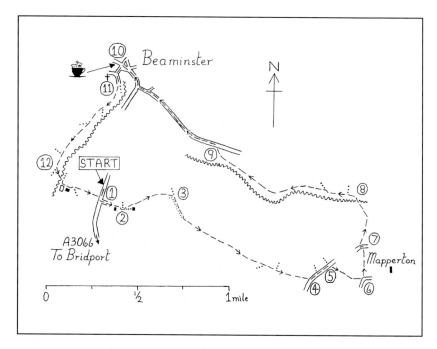

were usually buried at nearby Netherbury because the ground was too rocky in their own churchyard. During the plague, Netherbury would not accept the corpses so they were buried on Warren Hill, on your right as you walked along the track.

As Mapperton was wiped out by the plague, it is now no more than a hamlet with a fine manor house. This was built by Robert Morgan in 1550: he was one of the few men allowed to wear his hat in the presence of the King, 'in consideration of the diverse infirmities he hath in his hedde'. One wonders what they were! Only the north wing of the original house remains and the appearance today is more typical of the 17th century. You may feel it is familiar; it has been used as the location of several films including 'Tom Jones' and 'Emma'. The beautiful gardens are open daily from 2pm to 6pm between March and October (telephone: 01308 862645).

4. Turn left for about 180 yards, to the bottom of a small dip.

5. Turn right through a metal field gate. The right of way goes across the field in the direction shown by a sign but at the time of writing this had not been reinstated and there is an easy way to the left round the edge of the field to pick up the path just to the right of three trees. Continue along the path to a lane.

The Posy Tree near Mapperton

6. Turn left immediately through a metal field gate and across a field to another lane.

7. Turn left for 25 yards then right into a field. Head half right to the far right corner. In the next field head half left, downhill, to a stile. Over a stile, go ahead across a wooden footbridge over a stream.

8. Turn left to walk with the fence and stream on your left down a valley on a barely visible path. After a bare ½ mile, you have to bear right uphill and away from the stream to a gate in a boundary fence. Through the gate, the path is much more obvious. Follow it from gate to gate, passing an oak of enormous antiquity, to a drive. Turn right to a road.

☕ **9.** Turn left into Beaminster, passing the museum. At a main road, turn right into the square and continue ahead into Hogshill Street to the teashop on the left.

Beaminster (pronounced Bemm'ster) is a most attractive town and well worth taking the time to explore. Set in a bowl of green hills, it originated in Saxon times. Part of its appealing appearance is due to most buildings being constructed of the local creamy-orange limestone and many dating from the late 17th or early 18th centuries. It was devastated by fire three times in 200 years. The fire of 1644 was particularly destructive. It was during the Civil War and some Royalist troops under Prince Maurice were quartered in the town. A dispute between soldiers led to the fire being started and an account from the time says the whole town was destroyed in two hours. To make matters worse, goods rescued from the fire were then plundered by the soldiers. When Fairfax marched through with the Parliamentary troops the following year, it was said to be: 'the pityfullest spectacle Man can behold, hardly a house left not consumed'.

10. Return to the square and turn right down Church Street. Turn left along St Mary Well Street to the end.

11. Turn right along a track, signed 'Brit Valley Way'. When the track swings left, carry on in the same direction on a path signed by arrows on a post across two fields to a gate.

Lieutenant William Barnard Rhodes-Moorhouse is buried on the hill to the right. He was the first airman to receive a Victoria Cross, awarded posthumously. Though severely wounded in a bombing raid in the First World War, he managed to fly his aircraft back to base at Merville where he died next day. He owned Parnham at the time and the hillside was a special place for him; he intended to build a summerhouse on the spot. The ashes of his wife, also a pilot, and his son, killed in the Battle of Britain, are interred there too.

12. Go through the gate and after 10 yards fork left through woods to a footbridge. Over the bridge, turn right then left through the car park and between the buildings of Parnham House. The house and grounds are private and there is a charge for visiting them. The signed route leads to a drive. Walk along this to the road and the start.

Parnham House is one of the most beautiful houses in Dorset in an idyllic setting. It was built in the 16th century on medieval foundations and was enlarged and embellished by Nash, the great Regency architect, in 1810. It is now the home of the John Makepeace Furniture Workshop where stunning modern furniture is made and displayed and craftsmen of the future are trained. Parnham House is open several days a week between Easter and October (telephone: 01308 862204).

Walk 19
STOKE ABBOTT AND BROADWINDSOR

This is a magnificent walk in one of the hillier parts of West Dorset. The route climbs out of the picturesque village of Stoke Abbott to Lewesdon Hill. There are extensive views to Golden Cap and the sea to be enjoyed before dropping down to Broadwindsor for tea. You will have a further short climb on leaving the village, rewarded with some more brilliant views from the path as it gently descends to Stoke Abbott.

 Redundant farm buildings on the edge of Broadwindsor have been converted into a Craft and Design Centre with a range of enterprises from hats through watercolours to gifts imported from Peru. The airy restaurant is partly in the buildings and partly in an attractive conservatory and has tables outside overlooking the courtyard with an enormous geode of purple quartz discovered in Brazil in 1991. A splendid selection of cakes and pastries is served along with some very tempting sweets and cream teas. There is a good choice for a light lunch including, for example, soup, filled jacket potatoes and various ploughman's as well as a hot dish of the day for a more substantial meal. Broadwindsor Craft and Design Centre is open every day between 10 am and 5 pm from the beginning of March until immediately before Christmas. Telephone: 01308 868362.

When the teashop is closed, the pub in Broadwindsor, the White Lion, and the one in Stoke Abbott, the New Inn, both serve food.

DISTANCE: 5 miles.

MAP: OS Landranger 193 Taunton and Lyme Regis or Explorer 29 Lyme Regis and Bridport.

STARTING POINT: Stoke Abbott telephone box (GR 453006).

HOW TO GET THERE: Stoke Abbott is signed from the B3162 Bridport to Broadwindsor road. There are several spots where a car can be left without causing inconvenience, notably at the side of the road to Broadwindsor, Norway (North Way) Lane.

ALTERNATIVE STARTING POINT: If you wish to visit the teashop at the beginning or end of your walk, start in Broadwindsor where there is a large car park at the Craft Centre, though permission should be sought before leaving a car for a long period. You will then start the walk at point 10.

THE WALK

1. With your back to the phone box, turn right and walk out of Stoke Abbott along a lane.

Stoke Abbott is a charming, unspoilt village with domestic buildings of every age from the 17th century onwards, many of which are thatched. Life in villages has changed much in the last century. The records show that 100 years ago Stoke Abbott was a largely self-sufficient community with its own rector, a school and shops. The parish lost its rector in 1949, the school closed in 1950, the shop and post office in 1979. Many of the residents now commute to work in nearby towns and some houses are holiday homes. In 1858 one of the houses was seen to be on fire. A young woman of 23, Sarah Guppy, was found on the floor with her throat cut. She and her mother lodged at the house with a labourer called Seale. The murderer was found to be James Seale, aged 20, the son of the tenant. He was described as 'a thin, ill-fed and wretched young person'. He had a poor reputation in the village and had already served four months on the treadmill for robbing a child of 1s 10d. He was hanged over the lodge of Dorchester Gaol, the last public hanging in Dorchester. The

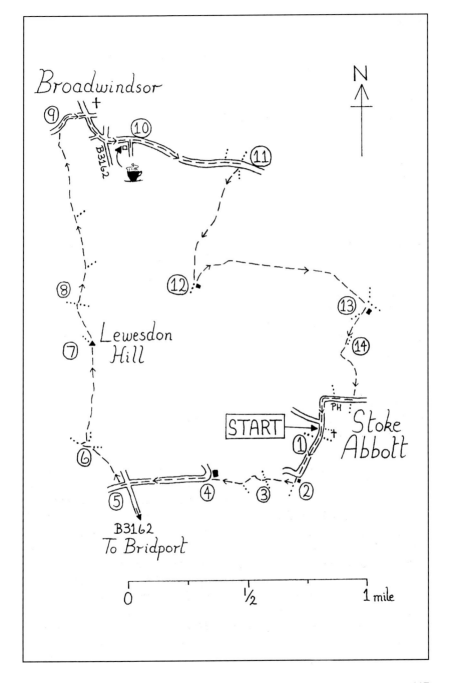

execution was watched by Thomas Hardy through a telescope and the experience profoundly affected him.

2. When the lane bends sharply right, continue in the same direction along a track to the right of a house for 50 yards. Turn right on a signed path through a field gate. This soon faded out at the time of writing but press on in the same direction, passing to the right of a small copse and on across a second field to a stile onto a track.

3. Walk straight across to go over a stile then down into a little valley to another stile on the right into a strip of woodland. Now head up the left-hand side of a field towards a farm. At the top, go over a stile and along a hedged path to emerge on a lane at the farm.

4. Turn left. Cross a main road and continue along the lane for 35 yards.

5. Turn right through a field gate and head very slightly left across a field to a second gate. Through (or over!) the gate walk half left towards the edge of a wood ahead to find another gate onto a concrete track. This path across the fields was not visible on the ground at the time of writing.

6. Turn left for 35 yards then right through a field gate on a path into woods. After about 50 yards turn left again on a clear path. Climb up through the woods, initially with a field on the left and then a bank. At a gap in the bank, veer right to avoid fallen trees to meet another bank on the right. When this ends, take a path uphill ahead, by a National Trust sign, to the top.

This is Lewesdon Hill. Its 894 feet give wonderful views; slightly west of south is the back of Golden Cap, less distinctive from this direction. This summit was the favourite spot of one of Stoke Abbott's 18th-century parsons, William Crowe. He climbed up here one day in May and wrote what Wordsworth thought was an admirable blank verse poem about his feelings, which many will share:

> *'Above the noise and stir of yonder fields*
> *Uplifted on this height I feel the mind*
> *Expand itself in wider liberty.'*

Crowe was the son of a Winchester carpenter and won a scholarship to Oxford. He became public orator for the University: it was his job to give speeches in finely turned Latin. He was so poor he used to walk to Oxford to carry out his duties, carrying his clothes over his arm and composing his oration as he went.

7. Fork right and continue on the path down the other side of the hill to a cross track.

8. Go over the cross track to a stile into a field and walk along the left-hand side then continue across four more fields to a gate onto a track. Carry on along the track to reach a lane.

9. Turn right into Broadwindsor. Turn right again at a crossroads and continue for about 1/4 mile through the village, taking the B3163 towards Beaminster to the outskirts of Broadwindsor. Turn right at Redlands Road to the teashop through the car park at the Craft Centre.

Some 40 cottages and houses in Broadwindsor, most of them dating from the 17th century, are listed as of historic interest. In the centre of the village, at the crossroads near the church, one cottage has a plaque stating that Charles II slept here on the night of 23 September 1651. I don't expect he got much sleep because he was pursued by Parliamentary troops and was trying to flee to France after his defeat at the Battle of Worcester (see walk 20). It is said that he escaped because the troops' attention was distracted by one of their camp followers giving birth.

10. From the teashop turn left back to the road and right along it for about 1/2 mile.

11. Just before the brow of a hill turn right through a wooden field gate. Do not follow the obvious track but bear right immediately, at the time of writing through a ramshackle wire fence, down to a gate in the far right corner. Now continue along the right-hand side of two fields, the left-hand side of a third and the right-hand side of a fourth to a gate into a farmyard with dilapidated and rusting corrugated iron buildings.

12. Through the gate, turn immediately left through another gate along a track leading up to two gates. Go through the one on the right and walk along the left-hand side of three fields then along a broad, grassy track to a house in a wonderful position.

Waddon Hill, to the right of the track, was the site of a Roman fort built during the invasion in AD 43 and probably held by the Second Augustan Legion. During quarrying in 1876 and 1878 some Roman coins and pottery turned up but the most important find was an iron scabbard with gold alloy inlay from the first century AD. It is now in Bridport Museum. A full excavation was carried out in the 1960s that showed the fort was constructed of wooden buildings set in slots carved in the limestone. It was only occupied for about 10 years, after which time it was no longer needed. The archaeological evidence shows the demolition was carried out in an efficient, military manner with the buildings removed and the site left in a tidy condition.

13. Turn right through a small wooden gate and go ahead to a metal gate, ignoring a more obvious path bearing right. Follow the level path with magnificent views to the left. This leads to a drive.

14. Turn right to reach Stoke Abbott then turn right through the village, back to the start.

Walk 20
CHARMOUTH

If you have over-indulged in cream teas and need to burn off some calories, I cannot recommend this outstanding, energetic walk too highly. The main problem is likely to be getting going! The route starts at Charmouth foreshore, a paradise for anyone interested in natural history. The beach below the crumbling cliffs is well known as one of the premier spots for fossil hunting and a wealth of shore life is revealed at low tide. The walk heads east along the cliffs then climbs the appropriately named Chardown Hill before returning inland on a high level route. The scenery is some of the best in Dorset with extensive views of Golden Cap and the rolling West Dorset countryside.

Any good resolutions you may have are likely to be undermined at the Garden Room at Kingfisher's. It is an outstanding tearoom in, as its name suggests, a conservatory overlooking an attractive garden which also has some tables. The cook's daily selection of cakes is offered and with a cream tea you can choose what sort of scone you would like — fruited, plain or wholemeal. For a light lunch, sandwiches and baguettes are available with some interesting and innovative fillings such as chicken, bacon and sweetcorn with pepper sauce. Salads include a Greek variety with feta cheese and olives and avocado and prawn. For a more substantial meal, several different pies are offered such as steak and kidney or, for a vegetarian choice, broccoli, leek and mushroom. The Garden Room is open every day from 9.30 am until 6 pm between March and the end of October. Telephone: 01297 560232.

When the teashop is closed, there are several pubs and cafés in Charmouth which serve food.

DISTANCE: 5 miles.

MAP: OS Landranger 193 Taunton and Lyme Regis or Explorer 29 Lyme Regis and Bridport.

STARTING POINT: Charmouth foreshore car park (GR 365930).

HOW TO GET THERE: Charmouth lies just off the A35 Dorchester to Lyme Regis road. In the town, follow the signs to the beach car park.

ALTERNATIVE STARTING POINT: The teashop is on the way into Charmouth from the A35 (approaching from Bridport), and close to the end of the walk. If you wish to visit the teashop at the beginning of your walk, the best bet is to find a spot to park on the road close by. You will then start the walk at point 6.

THE WALK

The first complete fossil skeleton of an ichthyosaurus was discovered in the cliffs just to the east of Charmouth in 1811. Mary Anning, a Lyme Regis schoolgirl, spent some eight years digging it out and received £23 for her efforts. The fossil is now in the Natural History Museum in London. She went on to make her living as a fossil collector. The family's fossil shop was visited by the King of Saxony who thought £15 a very reasonable charge for a superb ichthyosaurus embedded in clay. He asked Mary for her name and address for future reference and, as she handed it to him, she assured him, 'I am well known throughout the whole of Europe'. As the cliffs crumble, new treasures are always being revealed among the fallen rocks on the beach below. The ledges running out to sea are an excellent place to study shore life at low water. The Charmouth Heritage Coast Centre, to the right of the car park, is well worth a visit. They have excellent displays and run fossil-hunting seashore walks. Admission is free and they are open every day between 10.30 am and 5 pm during the summer from the end of May until the end of September and at Easter and during the October half term (telephone: 01297 560772).

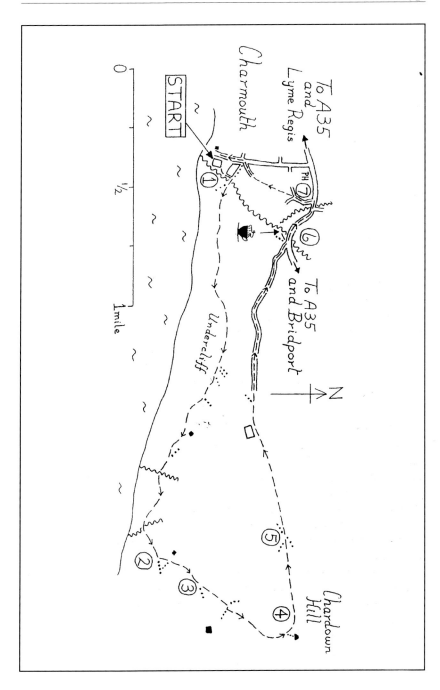

Charmouth foreshore and cliffs.

1. Facing the sea, go out of the left-hand side of the car park to a bridge over the river Char then follow the clear path, signed 'Seatown 4', ahead up the cliff. At the top, continue along the coast path for the best part of a mile, passing to the right of Westhay Farm and crossing two streams at footbridges. Climb the next hill.

This walk is mostly within the Golden Cap Estate, owned by the National Trust. Geologically, the area consists of limestone and clay layers laid down during the Jurassic era. On top of this is a layer of greensand; much of it has been eroded away but some remains as a cap on the hills. Perversely, the greensand is a rich, golden orange and is exposed on the seaward side of the cliffs, as you can see ahead during your ascent. Golden Cap itself is 618 feet above sea level, the highest cliff on the south coast of England. As mentioned above, these cliffs are constantly crumbling away and land slips and cliff falls form the undercliffs, rich in wildlife. The first cliff climbed is called Cain's Folly but who Cain was or what was his folly is not clear; presumably Cain was foolish enough to construct a building which disappeared over the cliff. In relatively recent times, the name was given to a clump of beech, now gone. If you look over the cliff at the top of Cain's Folly, you will see the remains of a radar station which fell with the cliff on 14 May 1942. The surprised but unharmed RAF crew walked out when it came to rest.

2. At the top, turn left, signed 'Stonebarrrow Hill Morcombelake'. Walk with a hedge on the right, passing above a barn.

The estate is managed for wildlife and landscape quality. Farming is an essential part of this management as grazing maintains the herb-rich meadows and hedgerows that support a diverse population of insects and birds. Traditional farming methods are used and the difference between this estate and the farmland around, especially in spring and summer, is graphic evidence of the impact of modern agriculture on wildlife.

3. When the chimneys of a farmhouse come into view, bear left away from the hedge towards the top of Chardown Hill on a line shown by a fingerpost, the path not being visible on the ground at the time of writing. At a track turn right for 20 yards then left through a field gate to continue to the top of the hill.

4. At the top, bear round to the left, soon passing a bench, and continue along the top of the slope.

Much of this hill is invaded by gorse. This is kept in check by periodic burning to allow grassland flowers, and the butterflies and other insects that depend on them, to flourish. The area is only grazed in winter so the flowers can set seed.

5. At a junction of tracks, continue in the same direction, signed 'Stonebarrow Charmouth 1¹/₄'. Carry on when this becomes a surfaced lane to the teashop on the left at the bottom of a hill where the lane joins a road.

6. Return to the entrance and turn left along the road into Charmouth. Turn left along Bridge Road and walk to the end.

Charmouth was Jane Austen's favourite place. She referred to it as: 'sweet, retired bay, ... the happiest spot for watching the flow of the tide: for sitting in unwearied contemplation.' It has also seen its share of violence. In AD 833 the marauding Danes came in 35 ships and were only driven off after fierce fighting. Behind its 19th-century front, the Queen's Arms is a medieval building. Catherine of Aragon stayed here when she arrived in England in 1501. She wasn't in as much of a hurry as Charles II a century and half later. Following the defeat at Worcester, he was hiding on the south coast, trying to get away to France. Charles was travelling as the servant of an apparently eloping couple, played by Lord Wilmot and Juliana Coningsby. A Charmouth skipper had agreed to take them to France for £60.

However, his wife heard about the dangerous mission. Fearing for his safety, she stopped him making the rendezvous by locking him in his room when he called home to pick up some linen. The three passengers anxiously waited at the inn and decided that something must have gone wrong and left for Bridport. Charles and Juliana went first because Lord Wilmot's horse needed shoeing. The smith told the ostler the horse had previously been shod 'Worcester style'. The ostler alerted the parson, Bartholomew Wesley, an ancestor of the famous John Wesley, and together they went to the magistrate. The magistrate didn't believe them so the ostler went to the military at Lyme Regis, but by then Charles had gone away.

7. At Wesley Close, take a signed path to the left of a phone box. When the path ends continue in the same direction to emerge on the road just before the car park where the walk started.